"If you're like me, you devour Salt Han[...]
now you can devour his actual food. T[...]
happen to be looking for FLAVOR! Th[...]
eat every single recipe in this book."

—PHIL ROSENTHAL, *New York Times* **bestselling author of**
Somebody Feed Phil the Book

"Few things in this world make me hungrier than Salt Hank. He makes you want
to put your phone down, get in the kitchen, and create your own saucy, crunchy
masterpiece. Now, thanks to this exhaustive (and mouthwatering) guide, you can
finally bring the mustache home and taste it for yourself. That came out wrong.
Actually, you know what, no it didn't."

—ANDREW REA, *New York Times* **bestselling author of** *Basics with Babish*

"Salt Hank's cooking is genuinely impressive. It might seem like he's just making
sandwiches, but he has great technique and really bold flavors. I'd eat anything
Salt Hank offered me, with or without the bread."

—OLIVIA TIEDEMANN, **voted against Bobby Flay on** *Beat Bobby Flay*

"Beyond our social media rivalry and Salt Hank's unorthodox, Mario-character-
looking appearance lies an arsenal of truly incredible, must-try recipes in this
cookbook. Hank, you are a sandwich maverick, and these recipes more than
prove you to be a worthy opponent."

—OWEN HAN, **author of** *Stacked*

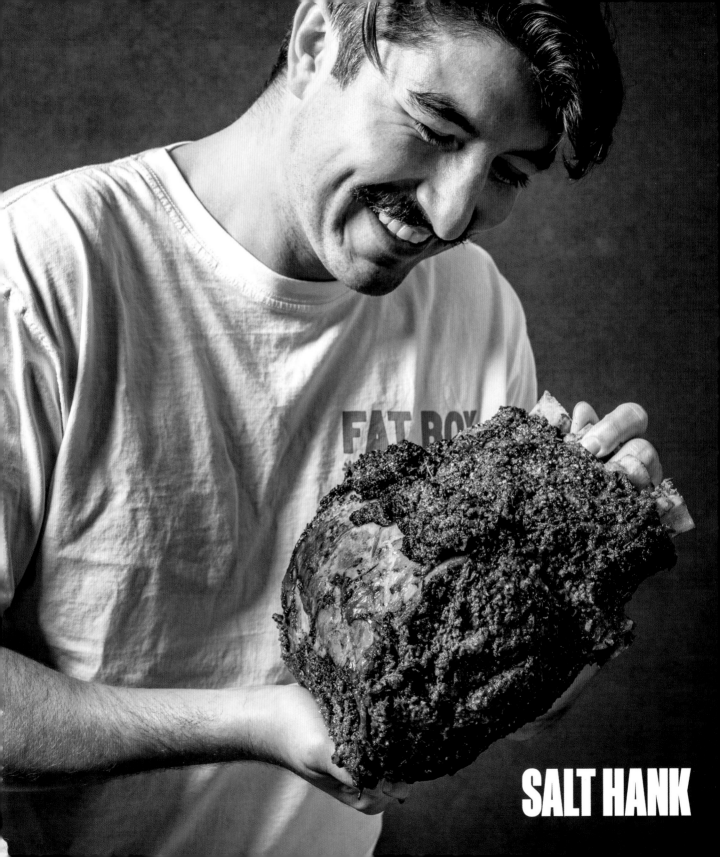

SALT HANK

SALT HANK

A Five Napkin Situation

Henry Laporte

with Ann Volkwein

Photography by Ed Anderson

SIMON
ELEMENT

New York London Toronto Sydney New Delhi

SIMON
ELEMENT

An Imprint of Simon & Schuster, LLC
1230 Avenue of the Americas
New York, NY 10020

First Simon Element hardcover edition October 2024

SIMON ELEMENT is a trademark of Simon & Schuster, LLC

Simon & Schuster: Celebrating 100 Years of Publishing in 2024

For information about special discounts for bulk
purchases, please contact Simon & Schuster Special Sales at
1-866-506-1949 or business@simonandschuster.com.

The Simon & Schuster Speakers Bureau can bring authors
to your live event. For more information or to book an event,
contact the Simon & Schuster Speakers Bureau at 1-866-248-
3049 or visit our website at www.simonspeakers.com.

Interior design by Laura Palese
Food Stylist: Lillian Kang
Assistant Food Stylist: Paige Arnett

Manufactured in China

10 9 8 7 6 5 4 3 2 1

Library of Congress Cataloging-in-Publication Data
has been applied for.

ISBN 978-1-6680-2548-2
ISBN 978-1-6680-2549-9 (ebook)

Dedicated to my family.
Love you guys.

Fried Foods and Appetizers

Main Courses

Sauces, Dips, and Salsas

Fermented and Pickled

Sandwiches and Burgers

ACKNOWLEDGMENTS

Everyone who helped with the creative side of this book deserves way more credit than I do for its existence. Ann Volkwein, Ed Anderson, Lillian Kang, Paige Arnett—I know there were moments where my disorganized brain put you all through hell, but you still managed to create magic with the cluttered recipes and notes I gave you, and I genuinely think we've created a masterpiece together, so I owe you all endlessly for that. Thank you from the bottom of my heart. Without you guys this would be iPhone pictures next to incoherent ingredients in a Word doc. You're all ridiculously talented people and I'm so lucky to have worked with you.

This book also wouldn't exist if it weren't for my wonderful manager, Ali Wald, who pushed me to go for it. Thank you for everything, Ali—I wouldn't be here without you.

A giant shout-out to my badass literary agent, Brandi Bowles, and my editor extraordinaire, Justin Schwartz. You guys might be a li'l bit crazy for believing in me, but I can't thank you enough, and I really hope people buy the book so we can potentially do this again together one day. Same goes for the whole team at Simon Element. Although I don't think I've even met some of you, I still love you all for making this happen.

Most of all my family. I can't imagine a more supportive, dysfunctional group of cheerleaders. Every day, it feels like their top priority is supporting me and my dreams. We've been through a lot of truly screwed up, hellish situations, but even throughout the bad stuff they have devoted so much time and love to me when I needed it. Abby, Mom, Dad, I love you all more than words can describe, and I am so unbelievably lucky to have you. Abby—to achieve what you've achieved after going through such hell is straight-up unbelievable. You're going to do great things and there is no way to describe the respect and love I have for you. Mom, you are the most compassionate, loving human in the world and a true champion for others. The world is a significantly better place with you in it and I can't imagine life without you. Dad, you are the smartest dude I've ever met and helped me make my first cooking video when I was like seven years old, which might be where this all started. You also gave me my first camera and my love for entertaining. My entire life and career are credit to you guys and the support you've all given me, and I love you all more than anything.

INTRODUCTION

First and foremost, thank you for even opening this book. I'm gonna get the corny stuff out of the way quickly, but it's important for me to note that you are the reason this book exists. You guys turned a fantasy that I've had since I was a kid into my real life and it's hard for me to believe that I'm writing this right now. I don't think I'll be able to fully express to you how grateful I am, or even process that this is actually real until years from now, but we did it, fam. Thank you guys forever; I love you all.

Second order of business, the entire point of this book is for the food to just taste amazing. That's the theme. I don't focus on whether it's healthy, nutritious, or hard to make. Flavor is the only priority for this book because that's how I genuinely cook. I don't care about anything else when I'm cooking. If there is a compound butter that doubles the calories in a sandwich but also doubles the flavor, without hesitation it's going in the sandwich. For me, that perfect bite is worth it.

Oddly enough, I can pinpoint the moment that philosophy took hold of my life. It was the first time I had salami. I was six (according to my mom) and standing in our kitchen. She handed me a normal-ass slice of salami. Hand to God it changed my life forever. I can't really speak to this, and I don't mean to offend here, but I imagine it was like doing heroin for the first time. Like there was this unfilled hole in my life and that slice of salami filled it. Since then, all my core memories throughout childhood are of bites of food that I took. I remember everything about those moments. The room I was in, the clothes people were wearing, the emotions I felt, all because the food sparked a bigger response in my brain than anything else ever came close to. Overall, I have a terrible memory, but when it comes to eating good food, I feel like Rain Man. So that's basically why my food and recipes are the way they are. I'm chasing the flavor dragon, and now you guys are chasing it with me.

That piece of salami changed the trajectory of my life in multiple ways. Like most kids, I had no idea what I actually wanted to be when I grew up, but without knowing it I'd already been groomed by food. One Valentine's Day in high school I convinced the dean of students to let me compete with the student counsel by selling salami grams instead of candy grams. We blew them out of the fucking water. I sold dozens of crappy little heart-shaped pieces of paper with hunks of salami taped to the front, and hand-delivered them during classes. This wasn't a shtick for me; I genuinely would just rather eat a salty, fatty piece of salami than a piece of candy, and I naively assumed other students would agree.

I didn't know it at the time, but it was the real beginning of my career in food. I had horrible grades and didn't really care about my classes, but for some reason I felt compelled to spend like a week preparing these salami grams. I just wanted to be around actual food and that instinct grew exponentially over the next few years.

SCREEN GRAB FROM ONE OF THE PROUDEST DAYS OF MY LIFE.

SALT MEETS FAT

I felt it was necessary to write a mini love letter on this. When these two things are combined, the flavor that they create is kind of my North Star. My love for them is what guided me into this career. I just figured this out while writing stories for this book—every defining moment in my cooking journey has mostly been because of the fat and the salt. My first bite of salami, the first time I had tri tip, eating the skin off my mom's roast chicken, it was the deeper flavor profile I was so in love with, the fat and the salt. I'm not going to pretend to be a nutritionist here or sugarcoat the fact that most of my recipes aren't the healthiest. But if I became a cook because of how much I love eating fatty, salty shit and then wrote a healthy cookbook, I'd be a straight-up fraud. I fucking love, *love* fat and salt. In my brain, they are the undisputed best duo of any category of anything in the whole world. My all-time favorite bite of food you can create is the crispy skin off a freshly roasted chicken with no seasoning other than salt. Of all these stories of my mom scolding me in the kitchen, the realest, most common one was when I would eat the skin off her roast chicken before we were actually served the food. It happened every time she cooked that meal. I couldn't get enough of that addicting combination. It's all you need in a lot of situations. Chicharron is another great example. Straight up just fat and salt. Buttered toast is basically only good because of the fat and salt you put on it. These are just my opinions obviously; some people eat just toast with nothing on it, but I have a feeling they aren't the people that bought this book. I have an inkling of a suspicion that you people all bought this book because, like me, you are in love with fat and salt. And that's okay. As long as we take decent care of ourselves, I genuinely think it's worth it to eat whatever it is that you crave sometimes. I know for a fact that when I die, I won't be saying I regret eating all that salami. I'll probably be asking for a piece of salami or choking on one and that's how I die. This is stream-of-consciousness writing, but I just decided that's how I want to die. Choking on a piece of salami . . . it would be a full-circle, beautiful moment, where the thing I loved most in the world eventually takes me out. Maybe you end up in some kind of salami heaven if that's how you die. I hope so.

HOW TO COOK INTUITIVELY AND MAKE GOOD FOOD

I should probably say the best way to get good at cooking is through making all the recipes in this book, but that's simply not true. I genuinely think the easiest way to get good at intuitive cooking and being creative in the kitchen is just to watch YouTube videos. If you don't already watch YouTube cooking videos, I'm jealous. To me that's like meeting someone who hasn't started *Game of Thrones* yet. Go watch Matty Matheson's first *Munchies* video where he makes a cheeseburger. Don't even follow along, just allow yourself to fall into a rabbit hole of entertaining food videos, soaking up information along the way. It's like watching a fun class that's built to be enjoyable and you won't get tested on it later. Little tidbit, for the aspiring content creators, if you don't enjoy watching them, you probably won't enjoy making them. Start with the greats—Chef John from Food Wishes, *Binging with Babish*, Matty Matheson, and just search for your favorite recipes by these guys. They've more than likely made several iterations of it. Watch them cook, and soak up what they're saying for entertainment before bed. Then hit the kitchen and make it with your heart, kinda checking if you're doing it correctly, but also fucking up a bunch of times by not really checking. Change their recipes to your own liking, add more garlic, add less sugar, get the pan scorching hot, and either make it amazing or screw it up a little. Then, eventually, nail something that you made from memory and feel a whoosh of satisfaction land on you like an airplane. Use your hand to grab the salt rather than a tablespoon. If you're not into YouTube videos, read the methods for these recipes but not the amounts and try to make them.

This is how I learned to cook, and it's so much easier than people think. Just pretend like you already have swagger in the kitchen. Smash the burger like you've done it a thousand times before. Throw stuff into hot oil that you think might be better fried, and salt it when you take it out. It probably is better—unless it has lots of moisture, then you might blow your house up. The kitchen is a genuine playground, and you can't ever really truly fuck anything up unless you chop a finger off or in fact blow that house up, so be careful too. But any cook worth their salt has some bumps, bruises, and burns, so don't be too careful. Cook with swag and be confident and watch food videos before bed.

THE IMPORTANCE OF SHARP KNIVES

A nice chef's knife is the most important piece of equipment in your kitchen. It will fully change the way you cook and just make your life better in general. It also makes you look like a badass when cooking. Spend like $140 and do five minutes of research and it will fully change the way you cook. It makes everything easier (and safer) and enhances that genuine swagger. If you're attempting to learn any good kitchen knife skills whatsoever, buy a chef's knife first. This isn't an ad, and I've actually never spoken a word to this company, but it was my first chef's knife and is still my favorite many years later so screw it, free plug: get the eight-inch Mac Chef's Knife with Dimples. It's $140, you can buy it on Amazon, and if you hone it and take good care of it (wash and dry after every use) it will last you for years.

Watch a YouTube video on knife skills, and with your new skills you'll be an everyday Gordon Ramsay. There are really only two things you need to learn before knowing the basics of good knife skills, and with a sharp knife neither should take long to master: (1) the claw thing and (2) the way you grip the knife. You'll need visuals to learn these, so once again, hit YouTube. Josh Weissman has a great video on this, but there are also a thousand that all teach you the same stuff. This is truly the most important thing in your kitchen. Dull knives are a huge pain in the ass and actually dangerous to use. Get a great knife and I promise you won't regret it.

FOOD PORN

I didn't wanna do too much talking (writing) in this book; the visuals need to lead. Salt and fat are what got me cooking, but food porn is what got me making content. That's why the format of my videos is like 5 percent me making some dumbass comment and 95 percent close-up shots of indulgent-ass food. None of this is to say I don't dig into more personal details than normal here. I've done my best to lay it all out there, but I also want the food to speak for itself. When we finished the first day of photography for the book, I knew we were onto something special. The food porn in here is un-fucking-believable. In my brain it perfectly captures the over-the-top, go-crazy nature of my recipes. All of that and more is credit to my photography team, Ed, Lillian, and Paige. They made these photos happen, and I can't thank them enough for bringing the food to life in the way that they did. I know I'm just bragging about my own cookbook, so I'll shut up soon, but it really was content like this that made me first shoot food videos and pictures. If you scroll down to the very bottom of my Instagram page, you'll see a couple failed attempts to get pictures like these. It only took seven years to finally make it happen.

MAKING SHORT FORM FOOD CONTENT, USER'S MANUAL

I bet some people out there bought this book strictly for this little anecdote. To those people, I promise to fit as much info in here as I can think of and help you as much as I can. First thing to note, there are a thousand ways to attack this, but I only know mine. Every content creator you've ever watched has a different workflow and opinion. In light of that, I can only offer a couple subjective common denominators for what, I think, makes for high-quality short form content. Tiny summary if you're already bored: if your food is uniquely better-looking than other people's, it will stand out regardless of the production value. I think people sometimes focus more on their equipment than on the food they're making. Second thing to note: if your production value is uniquely poor, it won't matter how awesome your food is. So you definitely have to put in work on both sides before anything sexy pops out. You don't have to make content to survive, so you might as well start with the cooking part. For that, see what I said earlier about learning how to cook intuitively. It comes before this section for a reason, by the way; you have to at least kind of know how to cook first. Which isn't that hard—and BTW, most of my advice in that section is to watch YouTube videos.

Okay, now that you've addressed the cooking part and know your way around the kitchen, let's make some fuckin' content. Here are six key components that I focus on when making a video. By the way, you could write a thesis on each one of these, but I'll try to keep it short and sweet, mostly because I'm still an idiot about most of it and only know what I've learned through trial and error.

Last thing—all of these components are adjustable to your own liking. Starting out, maybe just try to keep the food tasting good, the shots in focus, and everything lit up, but as your technical ability becomes more second nature you can start to take way more creative freedom with everything. I'll describe some aesthetic decisions you can make as well, but focus on the basics in the beginning.

LIGHTING
TEMPO
AUDIO
FRAMING OF YOUR SHOTS
AESTHETIC FOOD
PATIENCE

Lighting

This is first because it's probably the most important. Your lighting affects every other automatic setting on your camera, so if you're shooting on your iPhone or with automatic settings on a camera, the footage is going to look shitty if it's not lit up. Or, if your camera doesn't adjust to the light, it'll be dark. You'll either need sunlight, LED lights, or a hybrid of the two. If you just turn on every light in your kitchen, it'll probably look orange, cast unwanted shadows, and still not be enough light to control your camera settings effectively.

NATURAL VERSUS ARTIFICIAL

Natural light comes from the sun. If you happen to have great natural lighting in your kitchen, congratulations—it's impossible to find a kitchen like that, so you've already won the lottery. If you don't, you can kinda fake it too (skip to next paragraph). When I say great natural lighting, I mean like the whole wall is a window and the sun is directly lighting your food up. Even if you have this window wall, you'll probably need to supplement it with artificial light at some point.

Artificial lighting is using anything other than the sun to light your footage. My recommendation for this is to use a couple LED panel lights on tripods with soft boxes. You can google mine for an example of what that is—Aputure's Amaran P60C panels. These are pretty nice, but you can find much cheaper stuff on the internet that won't look much different if you're doing everything else right. I usually just try to light up the food as much as possible, but you can get moody and aesthetic with the shadows if you want. If you shine your light from one direction, you can re-create sunshine by casting a shadow in the other direction. If you want everything to look well lit and normal, set your lights up on both sides of your camera, pointing directly at the food. These angles are your best chance of avoiding shadows. Set your Kelvin degree to 5600K. If you turn it up past that, your footage will look blue, and if you turn it down, your footage will look orange. Your kitchen lights are probably set much lower than 5600K, which is why your footage will have an orange tint if you film with them. I'm not gonna get into all the science behind the light spectrum, but you can google it if you're curious about what I'm talking about.

Tempo

This mostly applies to ASMR-style videos, but it's also relevant in all short form content. Try to figure out a good tempo for your video and stick to it. The rhythm of your video should somewhat resemble the beat in a song. It doesn't have to actually make a beat, but the speed and length of the clips should have some consistency for each chunk of the video. Like a song, the sounds or clips can go twice as fast, or twice as slow, but not completely off beat. In music, this is referred to as beats per minute (BPM). If the clips are all different tempos, the video will confuse the viewer. Like listening to a live band where the bongo player has zero rhythm. It's obviously a bit different, and you can get away with a lot more since it's not just audio, but I think this is just another way to get creative with your video. Samseats is probably the best when it comes to this. Go check out his content and close your eyes when watching. It's all very rhythmic and probably adheres to a BPM of sorts.

Audio

This might be the only one where you can't take a ton of creative freedom. Simply just don't have subpar audio. Or don't use your audio and put music over it. I use a shotgun mic and it works great. If you're on a camera, using a shotgun mic is the easiest solution. If you're using your phone, lavalier mics allow you to plug a receiver into your phone and put the mic wherever the audio is happening. Just search "iPhone lavalier mics" and there should be a million options. Mics are pretty easy to figure out, so just buy one that fits your needs and learn how to use it.

Framing of Your Shots

This basically describes what's visible within the boundaries of your shot. Like lighting and tempo, you can get moody and aesthetic with this, or be very neutral and just center your subject in the middle of each shot. Starting out maybe just try the latter. You can even set up one good-looking shot and keep your tripod and camera in the same place for the whole video, switching out your subjects. There are things like the rule of thirds that you can look up, but just try to be intentional with your framing. If something is out of focus or out of frame, have it be an aesthetic decision you made rather than incidental.

For instance, in almost every video I've ever made, the subject has some room on the left side, and usually goes past the wall on the right. I think that stemmed just from me being right-handed, but that framing decision has soaked into all of my shots regardless of what's showing on the right. That's become an aesthetic consistency for me that I ended up liking a lot. The off-kilter-to-the-right decision is just a tiny detail, but it makes a pretty big difference in my opinion.

Aesthetic Food

The presentation of your food matters more for content, and one of the main things you can do to spruce up your presentation is to make sure there's a wide spectrum of colors happening. Typically, in a sandwich video I'll try to include a protein, vegetable, carb/fried item, sauce, and garnish. With all these ingredients it's not too hard to include two or three color variations, but if you're just making fried chicken or something, sometimes it can look a little barren. The fried chicken in this book, for instance, has a buffalo honey glaze and a pickled onion/pepper garnish. For all intents and purposes color and flavor, these additions make it a better-looking and better-tasting dish. A few simple tricks I like:

- **Chives and green onions**—They always work as a garnish if your dish is lacking some color. If sliced lengthwise and soaked in a bowl of ice water, they will curl up and you can add a beautiful mountain of green onion strings to your dish. Or thinly sliced and sprinkled, either one is a winning garnish. Also amazing when fried. Refer to the Birria Dip sandwich recipe (page 234) for fried green onions.

- **Pickled veggies**—Pickled onions or peppers have some of the brightest colors of any food. These will make your salads or sandwiches pop to an extreme.

- **High heat**—For meat or veggies, if you are trying to achieve some type of intense golden-brown color, you need to make sure your pan is incredibly hot. Use a lot of low-smoke-point oil—not so much oil that you are submerging and deep frying but enough to quickly shallow-fry your food at a high heat for the ultimate golden-brown crust. Applies to steak and broccoli alike. For food that will be searing in the pan for longer like chicken or duck, you can reduce the heat and slowly develop that color while it cooks.

- **Extra-virgin olive oil and freshly cracked pepper**—If the top of your dish is lacking in contrast, but it isn't the time for chives (maybe the last thing was an herb and the top is already green), a little drizzle of olive oil and some freshly cracked pepper work perfectly. For instance, basil leaves on top of a chicken parm sandwich look a bit uninteresting, but when drizzled with olive oil and seasoned with salt and pepper, they look like their own little meal.

- **Toasting your bread/buns**—This is essentially mandatory for the entire sandwich chapter. If you're doing it in the oven or on the stovetop, brush a thick coating of olive oil on your bread or bun, then toast. For extra flavor, rub a halved garlic clove on your toasted bread.

- **Sauce**—Always add some texture to your sauce especially for burgers and sandwiches. Chives work great for this purpose too. They turn regular mayo into a flavorful-looking sauce. Add Worcestershire, salt, and pepper and you'll actually have a great one. Or mix your mayo with some whole grain mustard and give yourself an easy, textured mustard mayo.

A final thought, all of these things happen to make your food taste better too. It's not just a happy coincidence that all this shit looks good; our brains are telling us something.

Patience

Nailing all of this for every single shot is incredibly hard to do. Almost every video, I still have throwaway shots that are out of focus or framed poorly. Here are a couple ways to hedge your bets when filming:

- **Film each shot multiple times**—I make two sandwiches every single time I make a video, and usually use a combination of clips from both. When I'm chopping an onion, I usually get it from a couple different angles and chop it at a couple different speeds. Etc., etc., and then you have options if one shot looks bad.

- **Check your mic levels**—Make sure your audio isn't peaking or too quiet. If the audio is blown out, it's unusable.

- **Move slowly**—If you rush to set your camera up for the money-shot cheese pull, you'll probably end up with a great cheese pull, but a crappy shot. Don't let the visuals of the food rush you when it comes to setting up your lights and camera correctly. I've filmed so many out-of-focus intros because I wanted the food to be steaming hot when I turned the camera on, and the footage was completely wasted.

Doing this correctly takes a ton of time. These videos usually take four to eight hours to film and another three to five hours to edit. For some people, I'm sure it takes a lot less time, and this varies a ton depending on the food and type of content you make, but no matter what, it's an incredibly detail-oriented hobby and requires a ton of patience.

Okay, that's it. Have fun!

FRIED FOODS AND APPETIZERS

Going Deep, Frying

Since almost everything I make includes fried shit, I figured I should include a little note on the different approaches you can take to frying. I basically learned all this through a lot of trial and error, aka grease fires and scorched body parts, so apologies if the techniques aren't what you'd learn in a culinary school. They're more of a user's manual on how to not burn your house down while making crispy-ass food. Anyway, I'm gonna walk you through the main things I've learned as a guy who likes it fried.

DRY BATTERING

My typical (very common) dry battering method is as follows: coat your ingredients in plain flour, then egg wash or buttermilk, and finally your seasoned dry batter.

Dry batter frying is one of my favorite ways to cook. (It's also the reason I can't get rid of this dad bod. Worth it.) First of all, you're much less likely to screw up a dry batter than a wet batter. Wet batters require pretty specific measurements in order to achieve the crust you're looking for. For dry batter, you basically just throw shit in flour and fry it.

My rule of thumb for seasoning your flour: 1 tablespoon of each seasoning per cup of flour/bread crumbs/starch. For instance, with 1 cup of flour, you'll need 1 tablespoon of *each* of your seasonings. Garlic powder, onion powder, paprika, cayenne, salt, and pepper are a great, standard dry batter mix. Feel free to add whatever else sounds good; those are just my basic-ass seasonings, but you can throw in dried herbs, cumin, harissa powder, or whatever the fuck else you want!

When it comes to the base of the dry batter itself, you usually have four options: flour, panko, some other kind of starch, or a hybrid of those three. You can also crush a bunch of Cheetos or something and batter with those, but that's already probably in someone else's book.

- **Flour**—Basically any type of frying requires flour, so you might as well have some available just in case. This is my go-to for frying foods. After some practice, it requires the least amount of effort for a great outcome. It's also sometimes the only battering station you need. Fried onion strings start with ⅛-inch sliced onions, for example, which already have enough moisture on the outside that you can skip the whole three-step dredging process and toss them directly into your seasoned flour. Mind you, this will be a light coating, so if you want a thicker, chunkier crunch, soak them in some whole milk first, and then add directly to your seasoned flour. Typically shooting for 350–375ºF is a good range for frying with flour. At 375ºF, you could perfectly fry chicken, onions, shrimp, and pretty much fuckin' anything. You'll usually get a nice crunchy outside and perfectly cooked inside. I very rarely use a probe to check oil heat. Just throw in a piece of panko and if it starts to immediately fry, your oil's probably in a good spot. If it fries really violently and turns brown quick, your oil's too hot. To cool it down, pour a little more oil in or just turn the heat down and give it a couple minutes to cool.

- **Panko**—Always comes out crispy as shit. This is my go-to for tempura, chicken parm, or onion rings. It's probably the hardest to screw up, but sometimes it doesn't adhere well to your food after the egg wash, so make sure to show it some TLC when tossing it in the panko. Once the panko-battered item hits that hot oil, you should be fine, though. If you're frying vegetables, shrimp, or tenderized chicken, 350–375ºF is still a good general oil temp range. Panko will burn easily if the oil's too hot, so keep the burner over medium to medium-low.

- **Cornstarch or other starches**—These are perfect for holding up to outside moisture. If you wanna make a buffalo chicken sandwich that won't lose its crunch from the sauce, batter it in cornstarch. It's got kind of an odd color once fried, so if you don't plan on saucing it, maybe use a mix of starch and flour. It's also gluten-free for all my celiac lads out there.

- Frying meat is all about finding the right oil temp. The meat in question has to be perfectly cooked, while also achieving the perfect crunchy golden-brown outside. 365ºF somehow works pretty well for everything. Fried chicken will brown and cook through in 8 to 12 minutes. Shrimp tempura will do the same in like 3 to 4 minutes (panko batter crisps up quicker).

- Frying vegetables is basically just about getting the right color and crispiness of the batter, so you can raise your heat and just pull the veggies whenever your batter has reached a nice golden brown. You don't want to overcook the vegetable, so high heat and quicker cook is better in my opinion.

All this advice is assuming you don't have a deep fryer at home. If you have a halfway decent Dutch oven or a wok or basically any wide pot, you're golden. Even if you don't have a thermometer to check the temp, just heat the oil up over medium heat for 6 minutes and drop a piece of batter in. If the batter bubbles and starts to fry, your oil is hot enough.

Recommended equipment for this is a spider, or at least a large, slotted spoon to pull the fried foods out of the oil. Tongs work but can be kind of a pain in the ass if you're grabbing for a bunch of smaller fried items. Also, I probably should've mentioned this first, but you can only fry with *high smoke point oil*. You can shallow-fry in olive oil and it should be fine, just don't deep-fry with it. I use vegetable oil for deep-frying, but I know people are not big fans of seed oils, so if you'd like to splurge on some other high-end oil, just make sure it has a smoke point of at least 450ºF.

FERAL FRIES

I made these at home one time and lost my shit. They're almost identical to the ones from In-N-Out—but made with fries that are actually good. Also wanted to include this recipe 'cause I know most of you probably don't have an In-N-Out in your state. Now you can finally see what the hype is about.

3   Yukon gold potatoes
4   cups vegetable oil
     Kosher salt
6   slices American cheese
     Caramelized Onions (page 177), for garnish
     Feral Sauce (page 153), for garnish

Prepare a large pot of boiling water and a parchment-lined sheet pan.

Slice a thin section off the side of each of your potatoes so that you can lay them flat on the counter. Cut the potatoes lengthwise into ¼-inch slices or planks. Stack those and then cut ¼-inch fries, lengthwise.

Boil the fries until they are just becoming tender, about 5 minutes.

Drain the fries and spread them out onto the prepared sheet pan. Pat them dry and allow them to cool for 10 minutes. Place them in the freezer for 1 hour or until frozen.

Heat the oil in a pot or deep skillet over medium heat to 350°F.

Carefully add the frozen fries to the oil and fry, in batches if needed, until golden and crispy, about 8 minutes. If they don't seem crispy enough, just put them back in the fryer; it's basically impossible to overcook fries (unless you burn them). Set them aside to drain on paper towels and season with salt.

ASSEMBLY: Plate your fries and top with 2 slices of American cheese per serving. Place the plate in the microwave and cook on high until the cheese melts, about 1 minute. Top with Caramelized Onions and a big ladle of your Feral Sauce and serve!

FRIED CHICKEN

It took me years to nail fried chicken. There are so many different styles and methods, but one day while filming a video I just fuckin' nailed it. I was so juiced up and haven't switched the recipe one bit since then. (If you wanna watch the video, search for "perfect fried chicken Salt Hank" on YouTube.) Also, I'm not sure who declared that Buffalo Sauce was reserved for drums and flats, but slathering this sauce on a fried chicken thigh is a beautiful move. Then of course the pickles, veg, and ranch don't hurt one bit.

1	red onion, cut into ⅛-inch-thick slices
3	fresh serrano peppers, sliced into ⅛-inch-thick rounds or a bit wider
2	cups white wine vinegar
2	cups water
5	tablespoons kosher salt, divided
2	tablespoons sugar
2	cups all-purpose flour
2	tablespoons garlic powder
2	tablespoons onion powder
2	tablespoons cayenne
2	tablespoons paprika
2	tablespoons freshly ground black pepper
4	cups buttermilk
2	cups dill pickle juice
1	whole (4-pound) chicken, cut into 8 pieces
	Enough canola oil to fill half of your frying pot

FOR THE SAUCE

3	cups Frank's RedHot
¼	cup (½ stick) unsalted butter
3	tablespoons honey
3	teaspoons garlic powder
	Finely sliced fresh chives, for garnish
	Spicy Ranch (page 152), for serving

Put the onion and peppers in a heatproof container or bowl. Add the vinegar, the water, 2 tablespoons of the salt, and the sugar to a pot over medium-high heat and bring to a boil. Pour the hot brine over your onion and peppers. Set aside.

In a large shallow bowl, mix the flour with the garlic powder, onion powder, cayenne, paprika, the remaining 3 tablespoons of salt, and pepper.

Pour your buttermilk and pickle juice into a large bowl. Add the chicken pieces, making sure everything is fully submerged. Refrigerate and allow to brine for at least 2 to 4 hours.

Remove the chicken from the brine, let it drain for a second, and then immediately add it to your dry batter, working in batches. Aggressively toss your chicken in the dry batter, making sure to press the flour into the chicken. Lay the pieces on a wire rack to set.

Heat the oil in a large pot over medium to medium-high heat to 350–375°F.

CONTINUES

Carefully add the chicken to the oil and fry until golden brown, 8 to 12 minutes. Remove it and set it aside to drain on a paper towel–lined sheet pan.

MAKE THE SAUCE: In a medium saucepan over medium heat, combine the Frank's RedHot, butter, honey, and garlic powder. Let everything meld together and stir well.

Plate the chicken, then paint it with the sauce glaze. Garnish the chicken with pickled peppers and onions, and sprinkle chives all over. Serve with homemade Spicy Ranch.

SPICY DRUNKEN MUSSELS

First off, get good mussels. There is one company that basically dominates the mussel game, called PEI Mussels, and those are what I'd recommend. PEI stands for Prince Edward Island, the location where they are farmed. These mussels are top dawg for a reason. The ocean water in this area produces a mussel that's consistent in its sweet, clean flavor; they're nice and plump, and they're sustainably farmed. This isn't an ad; I've just bought other mussels and found that they sucked multiple times. Another sidenote, if the mussel is already open before you cook it, it's dead; throw it away. If it hasn't opened after you've cooked it, also throw it away. I'll let the actual recipe here do the talkin' as far as flavor, but I promise if you like this type of food, you will be very psyched about the outcome.

8 tablespoons unsalted butter, divided

½ pound spicy Italian sausage

½ cup minced Calabrian chili peppers

1 large shallot, diced

6 garlic cloves, thinly sliced

4 cups dry white wine; sauvignon blanc works well

Freshly ground black pepper

4 cups low-sodium chicken broth

2 pounds PEI mussels

½ cup packed fresh parsley leaves

Juice of 1 fresh lemon

Baguette, sliced and toasted, for serving

Heat 4 tablespoons of butter in a large pot over medium heat. Once the butter has melted, add the Italian sausage, breaking it up with your hands while adding so that each chunk is medium to small. Let that brown for a bit and release some of its fat, about 3 minutes. Break up any larger chunks with a wooden spatula. Then add the Calabrian chilis, shallot, and garlic. Cook, stirring constantly, until the shallot begins to become translucent, about 3 minutes. Add the wine and 3 or 4 cracks of pepper and stir well.

Bring the liquid to a boil over medium heat and reduce by half, uncovered, 8 minutes. Add the chicken broth and reduce by half again, 10 minutes. Add the mussels and cover. Shake the pot around, then let sit for around a minute, then stir the mussels with a large wooden spoon. Cover again and steam until the mussels have mostly all opened, another 1 to 2 minutes.

Add the parsley and the remaining 4 tablespoons of butter, then mix thoroughly again. Shake the pot around to make sure the butter emulsifies with the rest of the broth at the bottom. Pour the lemon juice over the top. Remove the mussels with a spider or slotted spoon and put in a serving dish. Keep an eye on the mussels, as they will shrivel up if overcooked. Discard any mussels that didn't open.

Put several ladles of the broth in your dish and serve with toasted baguette slices.

SPICY SALMON POKE

If you've had salmon poke, you probably assume that you know what this is gonna taste like (or so you thought!). It's not what you think! This poke uses our Sambal recipe, which elevates the flavor and the spice to a completely different echelon of dank. However, if you just want some standard-ass poke, no worries, just take out the Sambal.

¼   cup soy sauce

2   teaspoons Sambal (adjust for spice levels) (page 168)

1   teaspoon sesame oil

1   teaspoon rice vinegar

1   teaspoon honey

1   pound sashimi-grade salmon, cut into ½-inch cubes

½   cup thinly sliced green onion

½   cup pitted, peeled, and diced avocado

1   tablespoon Fried Shallots (page 75)

1   teaspoon toasted sesame seeds

Potato chips, for serving

In a serving bowl, whisk together the soy sauce, Sambal, sesame oil, vinegar, and honey.

Add the salmon, green onion, avocado, shallots, and sesame seeds and gently toss together in the sauce. Serve with potato chips.

BUFFALO SHRIMP

I dunno why this isn't on every appetizer menu in the world—OR ANY APPETIZER MENUS EVER. Why don't people make these?? Seriously, like if there's some weird reason that I shouldn't be making Buffalo Shrimp, let me know, but man, they're good. Sorry you can't find them at restaurants; it's unfortunate. But now you can make them yourself and your friends will be like omg, you're a genius.

1	cup all-purpose flour
2	large eggs whisked with 1 tablespoon water
2	cups panko
2	tablespoons Cajun seasoning
1	pound peeled and deveined jumbo shrimp
4	cups vegetable oil
	Kosher salt, for seasoning
1	cup Frank's RedHot
¼	cup (½ stick) unsalted butter
	Spicy Ranch (page 152), for serving
	Blue cheese crumbles, optional

BUILD YOUR BATTERING STATION: 3 bowls, 1 filled with flour, 1 with egg wash, and 1 with panko. Stir the Cajun seasoning into the panko.

Thoroughly coat your shrimp in flour, then dip them in egg wash and the seasoned panko. Make sure there are no dry spots.

Let the batter set for 5 minutes while you heat your oil.

In a large pot, heat the oil over medium-high heat to 375°F.

Carefully add the shrimp to the oil and fry in batches of five until golden brown, 2 to 3 minutes. Transfer them to drain on a paper towel–lined plate and immediately salt them.

To make the sauce, put the Frank's RedHot and the butter in a small pot over low heat until the butter has melted, then stir to combine. Brush the shrimp with the sauce.

Serve with homemade ranch, mixed with crumbled blue cheese, if desired.

LUMPIA

Lumpia is one of my perfect foods. It achieves the two primary goals of a truly good meal: texture and flavor. Immediately, biting into it, the crunchy exterior of the fried lumpia wrapper offers a huge amount of satisfaction. Then that flavor bomb of sweet chili sauce and savory, meaty filling hits you. The combination is such a beautiful thing, and it's not easily found, but lumpia nails it.

2   tablespoons extra-virgin olive oil
1   pound ground pork
1   cup peeled and shredded carrots
1   cup finely chopped cabbage
½   cup grated white onion
½   cup thinly sliced green onions
6   garlic cloves, minced
2   tablespoons soy sauce
1   tablespoon plus ½ teaspoon kosher salt
1   tablespoon freshly ground black pepper
1   package (about 25) lumpia wrappers
    (available at Asian markets)
1   large egg whisked with 1 teaspoon water
4   cups vegetable oil
    Sweet chili sauce, for serving

Heat the olive oil in a large pan over medium heat. Add the pork, carrots, cabbage, white onion, green onions, garlic, soy sauce, salt, and pepper, and cook, stirring constantly, until the vegetables are fragrant and the pork is partially cooked, breaking the meat down with your spoon, about 5 minutes.

Place 1 tablespoon of the pork vegetable mixture in the middle of the lumpia wrapper, a bit below the center. Fold the bottom corner up over the filling, fold the side corners in over the filling, and then roll your lumpia up. Use egg wash to seal it closed. Repeat this with all of your wrappers.

Heat the vegetable oil in a large pot over medium heat to 350°F.

Carefully add the lumpia to the oil, in batches, and fry until the outside is crispy and developing color, 4 to 5 minutes.

Serve with sweet chili sauce.

NOTE: You can also make this without precooking the filling, as the pork and veggies cook during the frying process.

PERUVIAN CEVICHE

This is a Peruvian-style ceviche that uses a tangy, milky liquid as the marinade. It's called tiger's milk (or *leche de tigre*) because it's believed to have invigorating and restorative properties. It's the meal that Charlie Sheen ate before he did that *60 Minutes* interview and claimed to have tiger's blood. It's a soupier ceviche, with a lot of excess liquid that I encourage you to drink when you're finished. Easily my favorite ceviche recipe.

1   **pound sea bass, halibut, or another firm whitefish**

2   **teaspoons plus a pinch of kosher salt, divided**

1   **cup packed fresh cilantro, divided**

1   **medium shallot**

3   **garlic cloves**

½   **tablespoon diced ginger**

1   **cup fresh lime juice**

½   **cup fish stock**

¼   **cup full-fat coconut milk (optional)**

¼   **red onion, thinly sliced, for garnish**

2   **fresh rocoto peppers (the bright red, cherry-shaped ones), thinly sliced, for garnish**

Flaky salt, for garnish

Potato chips or tortilla chips, for serving

Cut your fish into ½-inch cubes, reserving the thinner scraps for later. Put the cubed fish into a bowl and mix with a pinch of the salt. Place in the fridge to firm up.

Put ½ cup of the cilantro along with the shallot, garlic, and ginger into your food processor. Blend until minced, then add your lime juice, fish stock, reserved fish scraps, coconut milk (if using), and the remaining 2 teaspoons of salt. Blend for 30 to 45 seconds. Strain your blended marinade through a fine-mesh sieve, pushing all the excess liquid through with a large spoon. This process will take a couple minutes to ensure you've squeezed all the liquid out of the solids. (You can discard the solids.) This is your "tiger's milk."

Mix your tiger's milk with your fish and plate. Using a spoon, put all your fish in the middle of a serving bowl, then pour the leftover marinade on top.

Garnish with the red onion, rocoto peppers, remaining cilantro, and flaky salt. Give it a light mix and serve with potato chips or tortilla chips. Don't forget to drink the last bit of tiger's milk when you're done.

NOTE: Ask your fish purveyor for their recommendation that day on what's freshest. Also just cultivate a healthy relationship with your fish person in general. It might be one of the most rewarding relationships you end up having in life.

SPICY CAJUN SHRIMP

This is like having a mini seafood boil in a frying pan. You can apply this method to shrimp, lobster, mussels, crab, or almost any other shellfish. This is also a great time for you to just eyeball the amounts for the seasonings and aromatic ingredients. Since you're peeling the shrimp at the end, it'll be hard to over-season them, so go a little crazy with what you throw in the pan.

¼ cup (½ stick) unsalted butter

4 tablespoons all-purpose flour

4 garlic cloves, thinly sliced

¾ pound unpeeled jumbo shrimp

½ cup packed roughly chopped fresh parsley

Juice of ½ fresh lemon, plus more for seasoning

¾ tablespoon Tony Chachere's Creole Seasoning

¼ teaspoon red chili flakes

Some good bread to mop up the juices

In a large pan over medium-low heat, melt the butter, sprinkle in the flour, and add the garlic, then stir constantly until the mixture is smooth and reaches a blond color, 3 to 4 minutes. Raise the heat to medium and add your shrimp, parsley, lemon juice, Creole seasoning, and chili flakes. Cook, stirring constantly to coat the shrimp fully in the other ingredients, until just cooked through, about 4 minutes. Pour everything into a serving bowl. Squirt some additional lemon juice on top.

Suck the sauce off the outside of the shrimp peel and head, then peel the shrimp and wipe it around in the sauce. Enjoy with your bread.

PRO TIP: Bite the head off and chew/suck all the flavor out before spitting it out.

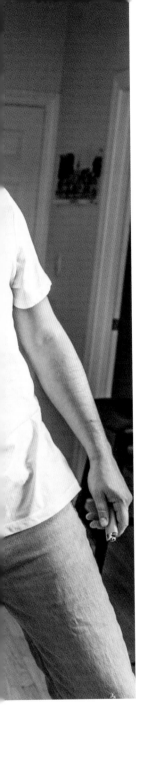

HASHBROWN PATTIES

I'm just gonna assume you've eaten one of these before in certain fast-food establishments, so you know how good they are. If you haven't, here's a spoiler—they're amazing. This recipe is obviously a bit more rustic and homemade, so in my opinion it's a vast improvement on the original. You be the judge. HEAVILY season with salt when they come out of the fryer. Trust me, they can take it.

3　　Yukon gold potatoes

½　　cup (1 stick) unsalted butter, softened

2　　tablespoons cornstarch

1　　tablespoon kosher salt, plus more for
　　　seasoning

2　　teaspoons garlic powder

2　　teaspoons onion powder

1　　large egg

4　　cups vegetable oil

Grate the potatoes over a cloth or napkin, then squeeze out as much of the excess liquid as possible.

In a large pan over medium-low heat, mix the butter with the grated potatoes. Cook the potatoes down, stirring occasionally, until they're softened and cooked through, around 10 minutes. Remove and let cool.

In a large bowl, mix the potatoes, cornstarch, salt, garlic powder, onion powder, and egg.

Shape the mixture into patties with your hands or with a 3-inch cookie cutter and place them on a parchment paper–lined sheet pan. Transfer to the freezer for at least 2 hours or until completely frozen.

Heat the oil in a medium pot or deep skillet over medium heat to 350°F.

Carefully add the frozen patties to the oil, in batches, and fry until golden brown, about 5 minutes. Transfer to a paper towel–lined plate to drain and immediately season with salt. Serve right away.

SHOKU'S CARAMELIZED ONION RINGS

If you're not aware of Shoku and their wizardly methods of cooking, allow me to introduce you. They're a small group of chefs who do exclusive private dinners for the rich and famous of Los Angeles. They have access to the rarest foods in the world, and turn these ingredients into fast-food-style delicacies like A5 Wagyu Truffle Philly Cheesesteaks or McDonald's-style Filet-O-Fish Sandwiches with Caviar Tartare Sauce. (They also serve dishes of incredibly refined gastronomy, but my favorites are the fast-food shit.) I've been lucky enough to cook with them a number of times, and one of the things we made was an A5 Wagyu Pastrami Melt with Caramelized Onion Rings. To make the rings, you blitz the onions, caramelize them, shape them into rings, freeze them, batter them, and fry them. If this sounds like a pain in the ass, that's because it is. Like I said, these guys are wizards.

FOR THE FILLING

4	white onions
¾	cup plus 2 tablespoons unsalted butter
2	tablespoons red miso paste
4	tablespoons Worcestershire sauce
2	tablespoons kosher salt
1	tablespoon freshly ground black pepper

FOR THE BATTER

1	cup all-purpose flour
8	large eggs, whisked
2	cups panko
4	cups vegetable oil or other neutral oil

Puree the onions in a food processor until they're almost a paste.

In a pan over medium heat, melt the butter and add the onions, miso, Worcestershire sauce, salt, and pepper. Gently stir to break up the miso paste. Continue cooking, stirring frequently, until the onions become dark brown and caramelized, 45 to 60 minutes. Remember to stir the onion mixture often to prevent burning or sticking; you're aiming to remove as much of the moisture as possible. The consistency is a bit like applesauce, and it has a tendency to splatter, so a screen helps if you have one. Once caramelized, remove the mixture from heat and transfer to a sheet tray or mixing bowl. Let it cool in the refrigerator.

Spoon the cooled onion mixture into a piping bag fitted with a ½-inch tip. Pipe the onion mixture into 2½-inch rings on parchment paper or nonstick baking mats. Freeze for 5 to 6 hours or overnight. They must be frozen solid.

Place the flour, whisked eggs, and panko in separate mixing bowls. Remove the rings from the freezer and coat them with the all-purpose flour. Coat the floured onion rings in the eggs and then the panko, ensuring they are fully coated. Repeat these steps with the eggs and panko to double batter the onions for extra crunch, and to ensure that the onion ring is completely coated and sealed to prevent the filling from leaking during frying.

At this point you can return the rings to the freezer and freeze for 2 hours. They can be stored frozen for up to 2 weeks.

Heat the oil in a large pot over medium-high heat to 375°F.

When fully frozen, working in batches, carefully add the onion rings to the oil and fry until the panko is golden brown, about 4 minutes. Set them aside on a paper towel–lined sheet pan as you go, until all rings are fried. Serve immediately.

NOTE: You don't *have* to make these; they're really fuckin' hard to nail.

TRUFFLE FRIES

If you ever want to seem fancy and distinguished, but also make something pretty simple and unhealthy, this is your dish. This is potentially the fanciest that French fries can be without involving caviar. Eat these hunched over your sink at midnight in your underwear and I bet you'll still feel kinda fancy.

1   recipe French Fries (page 66)
½   cup finely grated Parmesan, plus more for garnish
2   tablespoons truffle pâté (or truffle oil if pâté is unavailable)
3   garlic cloves, finely minced
2   tablespoons finely chopped fresh parsley, plus more for garnish
    Freshly ground black pepper
1   tablespoon extra-virgin olive oil, if needed
    Garlic aioli and ketchup, for serving

Put the freshly fried French Fries in a large mixing bowl.

In a medium bowl, mix your Parmesan, truffle pâté, garlic, parsley, and some freshly ground pepper. The final pâté should have enough oil that it's a thick dressing texture. If not, add some olive oil. Pour the mixture all over your fries and toss them up until all the fries are coated.

Plate on a serving dish and garnish with parsley and some freshly grated Parmesan. Serve with garlic aioli and ketchup.

FRENCH FRIES

3 Yukon gold potatoes
Lots of fine kosher salt
8 cups vegetable oil

Using a mandoline on the #2 setting, carefully slice your potatoes lengthwise. Stack your slices and cut them into fry shape with the same thickness as the mandoline setting (to the best of your ability). Do this in batches.

Lay your fries out on paper towels and season heavily from high above with salt. Let them sit for around 10 minutes, then pat them dry with more paper towels. Squeeze as much moisture out as you can.

Fill up a large pot or Dutch oven a little under halfway with your oil and heat over medium heat to 350°F.

Carefully add the fries to the oil and fry in batches until they turn golden brown, 3 to 5 minutes. Remove and let drain on a paper towel.

SERVES: 3
PREP TIME: 25 MIN
COOK TIME: 15 MIN
TOTAL TIME: 40 MIN

BONE MARROW

People call this God's butter. 'Nuff said.

6   marrow bones, cut lengthwise if possible

6   tablespoons extra-virgin olive oil, divided

1   teaspoon flaky salt, plus another couple tablespoons for garnish

½   teaspoon freshly ground black pepper

    Grated zest of 1 fresh lemon

1   baguette

2   garlic cloves

½   cup thinly sliced fresh chives, for garnish

Preheat the oven to 450°F.

Place the marrow bones flat side up on a sheet pan and brush them with 2 tablespoons of the olive oil. Season with the salt, pepper, and lemon zest. Roast for 15 to 20 minutes, or until the bones are slightly brown but haven't rendered too much fat.

While your bones are roasting, cut the baguette into slices, on the bias at a 45-degree angle. Heat the remaining olive oil in a large pan over medium-high heat, then shallow-fry the slices of bread until browned, about 3 minutes per side. Cut the garlic cloves in half and rub them on your baguette.

Remove the bones from the oven and serve hot with your crostini. Have flaky salt and thinly sliced chives available to garnish each bite.

BONE MARROW, PAGE 67

STEAK TARTARE

This is one of my death row meals. I love it so, so much. I won't be mad at you if you want to skip this because it's raw, but if you are raw meat curious, I encourage you to try it, especially if you like steak. I dunno if I can legally promise nothing bad will happen, but nothing bad will happen if you eat this. One time in college I accidentally ate raw chicken and now I'm writing a cookbook.

1   **(8-ounce) high-quality beef tenderloin filet**
3   **large egg yolks, divided**
1   **tablespoon finely diced shallots**
1   **tablespoon finely diced gherkins**
1   **tablespoon finely chopped fresh parsley**
1   **tablespoon thinly sliced fresh chives (reserve 2 halved chives for garnish)**
1   **tablespoon capers, drained**
1   **tablespoon red wine vinegar**
1   **tablespoon whole grain mustard**
1   **tablespoon Worcestershire sauce**
1   **tablespoon extra-virgin olive oil, plus more for frying**
1½   **teaspoons Tabasco**
     Pinch flaky salt, plus more for garnish
     Pinch freshly ground black pepper
½   **high-quality baguette**
2   **garlic cloves**

Put your steak in the freezer about 30 minutes before you start to cook. Cut your steak into ¼-inch strips, then cut those strips into ¼-inch strips. Dice up your strips of steak.

Put your diced steak in a large mixing bowl, along with 2 of the egg yolks, the shallots, gherkins, parsley, chives, capers, vinegar, whole grain mustard, Worcestershire sauce, olive oil, Tabasco, and a big pinch of salt and pepper. Mix everything up and put it in the fridge.

Fill the bottom of a large pan up with ¼ inch of olive oil and bring up to medium to medium-low heat. While the oil heats up, slice your baguette diagonally, as pictured. Working in batches as needed, fry until golden brown, about 2 minutes. Flip and cook until golden brown on the second side, 1 to 2 minutes. Remove to a paper towel–lined plate; repeat as needed. After the bread has cooled, cut your garlic cloves in half and rub the flat side aggressively on your crostinis.

Plate by filling a small round bowl with your tartare and then flipping it over onto your plate. Top with the remaining egg yolk, a big pinch of flaky salt, and your halved chives.

FRENCH ONION SOUP

We're going to use a little chef's cheat code here to fortify your soup. Instead of making your own beef stock, which takes an entire day, we're going to take store-bought beef stock and quadruple the flavor with mirepoix, bouillon, wine, Worcestershire, and salt. After deeply caramelizing our onions, we can add our fortified beef stock, reduce a little more and the base of your soup is done.

- 4   red onions, divided
- 2   white onions
- 2   yellow onions
- 4   shallots
- 9   tablespoons unsalted butter, divided
- 4   tablespoons extra-virgin olive oil, divided, plus more for brushing
- 1½ tablespoons kosher salt, divided, plus more as needed
- ½   tablespoon freshly ground black pepper, plus more as needed
- 1¼ cups Worcestershire sauce, divided, plus more as needed
- 3   cups dry red wine, divided
- 3   large carrots, halved and then cut into half moons
- 4   celery stalks, thinly sliced
- 1   tablespoon beef bouillon base, plus more as needed
- 12 cups beef stock
- ½   baguette
- 8   cups grated Gruyère cheese
- 1   cup thinly sliced fresh chives, for garnish

Start by thinly slicing all your onions. You need a mandoline or a sharp knife for this. Method for slicing: cut the root and tip off your onion, then cut in half, crosswise through the middle. Peel, then slice by following the natural lines in the onion. Reserve 2 of the sliced red onions.

Put 6 tablespoons of the butter and 2 tablespoons of the olive oil into a large Dutch oven over medium heat. Once the butter has melted, add your sliced onions (minus the reserved red). Season with ½ tablespoon each of salt and pepper. You are going to caramelize these over low heat for 2 to 3 hours, so this will require some patience; remember to stir at least every 5 to 7 minutes or your onions might burn. After they've picked up some color and are starting to create a fond on the bottom of the pan, add ¼ cup of the Worcestershire sauce and 1 cup of the wine to deglaze. Keep caramelizing until they've turned a deep brown color throughout and are very gooey.

CONTINUES

In a large saucepan over medium-low heat, heat the remaining 3 tablespoons of butter and 2 tablespoons of oil. Stir in your carrots, celery, the reserved sliced red onions, the remaining 1 tablespoon of salt, and 1 tablespoon of the beef bouillon base. Sweat your mirepoix, stirring occasionally, for 25 minutes, then add the remaining 1 cup of Worcestershire sauce and 2 cups of wine. Deglaze the pan, stirring frequently, and cook the wine completely off. Once it's cooked off, add your beef stock. Let this reduce by 30 percent or so, then strain the liquid and add the fortified beef stock to your caramelized onions.

Let reduce by another 10 percent, tasting as you go and adjusting levels of Worcestershire sauce, bouillon, salt, and pepper as needed.

Preheat the oven to 350°F.

Cut your baguette into crostini-size slices. Brush with olive oil and bake until golden brown and crunchy, about 20 minutes.

Fill a crock or ovenproof bowl with your soup, add a big handful of Gruyère cheese, 2 crostini slices, and another handful of Gruyère cheese on top. Repeat with remaining bowls. Place the bowls on a sheet pan and then under the broiler until the cheese is caramelized, deeply golden brown, and bubbling.

Garnish with your sliced chives and serve piping hot.

FRIED SHALLOTS

Easiest deep-fry recipe in this book. You can basically have the oil at whatever temp you want, and these will still come out perfect if you pull them when they're golden brown. We use these in Josh Weissman's Beef Bulgogi Sandwich (page 225), but put these on everything that might need a little boost. Anything savory could benefit from a fried shallot garnish. I especially like a delicate little appetizer where you can see just the one fried shallot on top. Love you guys, have fun.

4   **cups vegetable oil**
5   **medium shallots**
     Kosher salt

Heat the oil in a medium pot over medium to medium-low heat to 300°F.

While the oil is heating, thinly slice your shallots using a mandoline to ⅛-inch thickness.

Carefully add the shallots to the oil and fry until golden brown, 5 to 8 minutes.

Transfer to a paper towel–lined plate to drain and crisp up. Immediately season with a lot of salt after frying. Use on everything.

FRICKLES

In the words of Samin Nostrat, this is Salt, Fat, Acid, Heat. I can't think of a better way to celebrate these words than by making a gigantic platter of Frickles. Once again, season heavily with flaky salt and don't be shy with your ranch dips.

2	**cups all-purpose flour**
2	**cups buttermilk**
2	**cups panko**
2	**tablespoons Cajun seasoning**
6	**Quick Dill Pickles (page 193), cut into spears**
4	**cups vegetable oil**
	Flaky salt
	Spicy Ranch (page 152), for serving

Place the flour, buttermilk, and the panko mixed with the Cajun seasoning into three separate shallow bowls.

Dredge your pickle spears in the flour, then the buttermilk, then the seasoned panko.

Heat the oil in a large pot over medium heat to 350°F.

Working in batches, carefully add the pickles to the oil and fry them until golden brown, 4 to 6 minutes.

Remove to drain on a paper towel–lined plate and immediately season with flaky salt.

Serve with Spicy Ranch.

FRIED CALAMARI

The idea here is to make garlic fries but replace the potato with calamari. My favorite restaurant as a kid served it this way and I fell deeeeeeply in love with it. Also, those fried Pickled Peppers and lemon slices light this bitch on fire. Not in a spicy way—they just taste really good. Make sure to season *generously* with flaky salt before consumption.

2   cups all-purpose flour
2   tablespoons cayenne
2   tablespoons paprika
2   tablespoons onion powder
2   tablespoons garlic powder
2   tablespoons kosher salt
2   tablespoons freshly ground black pepper
1   pound calamari, bodies and tentacles, pre-cleaned and sliced
4   cups whole milk
4   cups vegetable oil
1   cup ⅛-inch-thick sliced fresh lemon
1   cup Pickled Peppers (page 201)
    Flaky salt, for seasoning
3   tablespoons minced garlic
1   cup packed fresh basil leaves
    Spicy Ranch (page 152), for serving
½   cup marinara of choice, for serving

In a large bowl, mix your dry batter of flour, cayenne, paprika, onion powder, garlic powder, salt, and pepper.

In a separate large bowl, submerge the calamari with the whole milk and let sit for a few minutes.

Heat the oil in a pot or deep skillet over medium heat to 350°F. Prepare a large paper towel–lined bowl.

Shake off some of the excess milk and toss the calamari in half of your dry batter to coat. Set aside. Toss the lemon and Pickled Peppers in the remaining dry batter.

Carefully add the calamari to the oil, in batches if needed, and fry until golden brown, about 3 minutes. Remove the calamari to a paper towel–lined bowl and season with flaky salt. Immediately add your minced garlic and toss.

Repeat with the lemon rinds and Pickled Peppers, frying in batches, if needed, until golden brown, about 3 minutes.

Finally, carefully add your basil leaves to the oil and quickly fry them for a few seconds—be aware that they will pop and sizzle, so stand back when you add them to the fryer.

Plate the calamari, lemon rinds, and peppers and garnish with your fried basil. Serve with Spicy Ranch and marinara.

FRIED LEMON SLICES

This one can freak people out because the rind is still fully attached, but like so many other things that are weird to eat raw (shrimp tails), once battered and deep-fried, they're amazing. *Sidenote:* You should try making fried shrimp tails at some point.

1	cup all-purpose flour
1	tablespoon garlic powder
1	tablespoon onion powder
1	tablespoon cayenne
1	tablespoon paprika
1	tablespoon kosher salt
1	tablespoon freshly ground black pepper
4	cups vegetable oil
4	fresh lemons
	Spicy Ranch (page 152), for serving

In a medium bowl, mix your dry batter of flour, garlic powder, onion powder, cayenne, paprika, salt, and pepper.

Heat the oil in a large pot over medium heat to 350°F.

Thinly slice your lemons with a mandoline to about ⅛ inch thick.

Immediately toss them in the dry batter, while the lemon slices are still fresh and moist.

Carefully add them to the oil and fry in batches until golden brown, 2 to 3 minutes, turning once.

Serve with Spicy Ranch.

FRIED CALAMARI, PAGE 78,
AND FRIED LEMON SLICES, PAGE 79

MAIN COURSES

SALT HANK

SOME OF THESE ARE INCREDIBLE, TASTY STUNT FOODS
and some of them are showstopping, classy-ass meals
that you could make the first time you meet your in-
laws. The Prime Rib Roast (page 121), for example, is
just a flawless representation of your cooking expertise.
If you have a meat probe and whipped compound butter,
it's easy to make but also wildly impressive. The ultimate
classy food. The rest are just incredibly tasty meals that
you maybe haven't tried before, so skim through all of
them and maybe pick out some favorites before you just
dive right in. Each of these is meant for a specific time and
place, so plan ahead. The Bang Bang Shrimp Tacos
(page 112) are a perfect party food, but as mentioned,
the rib roast will finally make your father-in-law respect
you. I don't wanna make this chapter intro too long
due to the massive variety of foods in here, so I'll leave
you with this—salt the absolute fuck out of everything.
Season everything more than the measurements say to.
Unless you have a fragile mouth, I guess.

HUEVOS DIVORCIADOS

This is one of the most creative methods of casual cooking I've ever seen. The recipe below is Salt Hank style, so it's filled to the brim with all types of delicious shit. You can doctor it up however you want, or you can minimize this to your liking. The only mandatory part is frying an egg on top of a crispy tortilla. Traditionally it's served with just the essentials, some salsa verde, cilantro, lime, etc., and that's how I would make it if I was cooking for a group. But with the carne asada, pickled onions, and more, it turns into something else entirely. I won't say better because I really am obsessed with the just-the-essentials version, but absolutely make your own and use whatever toppings you love. There's also an incredible moment when you're folding your crispy taco in half, and the yolk pops and oozes all over everything. I gotta shout out to my guy Freddster for putting me onto this technique.

	Carne Asada (page 89)
2	tablespoons vegetable oil
2	(6-inch) corn tortillas
2	large eggs
	Charred Red Salsa (page 171)
1	avocado, pitted, peeled, and thinly sliced
	Pickled Onions (page 191), for garnish
	Cotija cheese, for garnish
	Small handful of fresh cilantro leaves
	Tapatío or your favorite hot sauce, optional
	Squeeze of fresh lime juice

Cube the carne asada into ¼-inch chunks.

Heat the oil in a medium pan over medium to medium-low heat. Add your tortillas to the pan and let them sizzle and get crispy, about 2 minutes. Flip the tortillas, then carefully crack your eggs on top of the tortillas. Wait for 30 seconds, then add 1 tablespoon of water to the side of the pan and put the lid on. Let your tortillas crisp up and your eggs cook for another 3 to 4 minutes, then kill the heat.

Plate up with all the fixings: carne asada, red salsa, avocado, pickled onions, cotija, cilantro, hot sauce, if desired, and a squeeze of lime juice. Enjoy.

CARNE ASADA

1 cup orange juice
½ white onion, grated
½ cup roughly chopped, packed fresh cilantro stems and leaves
¼ cup soy sauce
¼ cup extra-virgin olive oil
4 garlic cloves, grated
1 fresh jalapeño pepper, grated
Juice of 1 fresh lime
1 pound skirt steak, or other protein
Kosher salt, for seasoning

In a nonreactive bowl, combine the orange juice, onion, cilantro, soy sauce, oil, garlic, jalapeño, and lime juice. Add your steak (or other protein). Make sure it's fully submerged so that the marinade is in contact with all sides. Marinate for 2 to 3 hours for steak.

Cook as desired or do as I do and get a pan ripping hot and add your steak directly from the marinade to the pan. Season heavily with salt and flip after 3 minutes; 3 minutes on each side should yield a medium rare steak.

Let rest and cube up.

MAKES: 2 CUPS MARINADE, SERVES 2
PREP TIME: 10 MIN PLUS 2 HRS MARINATING TIME
COOK TIME: 6 MIN
TOTAL TIME: 2 HRS 16 MIN

PASTA PRIMAVERA

This is verbatim my mom's recipe, so don't give me any credit when you have an out-of-body experience while eating it. It's one of my favorite meals of all time, so I didn't really see the point in changing anything. It's also one of the simplest recipes in this book, and it's ONE POT. Sorry, had to capitalize that 'cause it's probably the only time I'll ever be able to say it. This is an all-time comfort food for me, and I hope you guys love it. If not, take it up with Jennifer. Or don't, 'cause that's my mom and then we'd have an issue. Love you, Mama.

APPROXIMATE AMOUNTS FOR ALL

¼   cup extra-virgin olive oil

1   tablespoon plus 1 teaspoon kosher salt, divided

1   or 2 garlic cloves

1½ to 2 cups chopped ripe tomatoes

8   cups water

2   cups fusilli pasta

1   or 2 peeled and sliced carrots

1½ to 2 cups broccoli florets

Pine nuts, optional

Grated Parmesan, optional, for garnish

Freshly ground salt and black pepper

In a large bowl put the olive oil and 1 teaspoon of the kosher salt. Finely mince or press the garlic cloves and let sit while you chop the tomatoes. Add the tomatoes, stir, and smoosh. Set aside.

Bring the water to a boil, add the remaining 1 tablespoon of salt, then add the pasta, stir, and cook for 5 to 7 minutes; then add the carrots, stir, and cook 4 to 5 minutes. Watch to see when the pasta is nearly done, then add the broccoli, boil for 1 to 2 minutes, and turn off the heat.

Pour the pasta into a colander over the sink, swirl, and shake out any excess water, then rinse and jostle under tap water for about 5 seconds to prevent gluey pasta. Put the pasta back in the pot and mix in the olive oil, tomato, and garlic mixture. Stir, and if you're using pine nuts, add them into the mix. Serve hot, or at room temperature; garnish with Parmesan, if you like, and season with freshly ground salt and pepper.

MOM'S NOTES: You can use any vegetable, just watch how soon you add them to the pot; al dente is okay for this meal. It's nice if the vegetables have contrasting colors; it represents springtime, hence the name Primavera! Also, I specify kosher salt because it's the best for cooking. If someone uses table salt, the salt measurements would need to be cut almost in half (and it wouldn't be as good). And obviously the freshly ground salt is saved for the end. You've been eating this dish since you could chew!

NOTE: I made this in college a few times a week; it's really cheap, and delicious!

SALMON WELLINGTON

I stole this recipe from one of my mom's friends. I'd never heard of a salmon Wellington before, but immediately after trying it I remember going to the store to get the ingredients for a video. It sounds kinda fancy, but it's basically a cheesy spinach dip and salmon Hot Pocket. Fire.

6   tablespoons unsalted butter, divided

2   shallots, minced

6   garlic cloves, minced, divided

1   teaspoon chili flakes

1   teaspoon Cajun seasoning

½   teaspoon plus 3 pinches kosher salt, divided

½   teaspoon plus 1 pinch freshly ground black pepper, divided

3   cups packed fresh spinach

½   cup dry white wine

1   cup cream cheese

1   cup sour cream

½   cup grated Parmesan

½   cup Italian bread crumbs

1   sheet puff pastry, halved and rolled out

2   (7-ounce) salmon fillets, skin removed

1   fresh lemon, for seasoning, divided
    Flaky salt, for garnish

1   tablespoon chopped fresh parsley, for garnish

Preheat the oven to 400°F and line a sheet pan with parchment paper.

In a large pan over medium-low heat, melt 2 tablespoons of the butter. Add the shallots and 4 of the minced garlic cloves. Season with the chili flakes, Cajun seasoning, ½ teaspoon of the salt, and ½ teaspoon of the pepper. Cook, stirring constantly, until the spices are fragrant, about 1 minute, then add your spinach and cover. After 30 seconds take your lid off and mush your spinach down, mixing it with the other ingredients. Continue cooking your spinach down, stirring occasionally, until the leaves are mushy and soft, 5 to 7 minutes. Deglaze with the wine and let reduce for a couple minutes. Add the cream cheese, sour cream, Parmesan, and bread crumbs. Mix everything together until it is totally combined and melty, then remove from heat.

Make sure your puff pastry sheets are rolled out enough to be wrapped around your salmon fillets. Place your salmon in the middle and add a squirt of lemon juice on top. Season with a pinch of salt and pepper, then add a thick layer of your cheesy spinach topping to the entire top of your fillet. (Reserve any remaining filling and use it as a dip.) Wrap the fillet with the puff pastry, pinching all the seams closed on all sides, then flip over. Score the top of the puff pastry with 3 or 4 Xs, then season with another pinch of salt. Place on the prepared sheet pan and bake for 20 to 25 minutes or until the puff pastry is golden brown.

CONTINUES

While it's baking, make your garlic lemon butter. In a medium saucepan over medium-low heat, melt the remaining 4 tablespoons of butter and add the remaining 2 cloves of minced garlic. Once fragrant, about 2 minutes, whisk in a big squirt of lemon juice, a big pinch of flaky salt, and the chopped parsley.

You can straight-up eat this with your hands like a Hot Pocket, dipping it in the garlic butter. Or be fancy and use a knife and fork.

PALEO BOWL

If you thought this book was going to toss healthy eating to the wind and strictly focus on making the most delicious recipes possible, you'd be mostly right. Priority #1 will always be making the food taste amazing. However, if a healthy recipe happens to achieve that goal, I'm not going to leave it out of the book just to spite healthy food. I have no beef with healthy food; I just think it usually doesn't taste as good. This paleo bowl is one of those crazy anomaly meals that tastes insanely good and is still incredibly good for you. I legitimately feel like a better human, physically and morally, after eating one of these. And you will too.

1½   **cups quinoa**

½   **pound skirt steak**

1   **teaspoon kosher salt**

1   **teaspoon freshly ground black pepper**

2   **tablespoons vegetable oil, divided**

2   **bell peppers, thinly sliced (get 2 different colors)**

1   **white onion, thinly sliced**

2   **boneless, skinless chicken breasts**

1   **tablespoon Tony Chachere's Creole Seasoning**

4   **cups spring mix lettuce**

1   **cup Pickled Onions (page 191)**

1   **avocado, pitted, peeled, and sliced**

1   **cup Chimichurri (page 163)**

    Sriracha, for serving

Rinse the quinoa in a fine-mesh sieve. Bring 3 cups of water to a boil in a medium saucepan, then add the quinoa. Reduce the heat to low and simmer, covered, stirring occasionally until all the liquid is absorbed, about 15 minutes. Set aside.

Preheat the oven to 400°F.

Pat your steak dry and season heavily with salt and pepper. Heat a medium skillet over high heat for 10 minutes. Add 1 tablespoon of the oil and lay your steak down, away from your body as it is hot. Press down to ensure full surface contact. Wait 3 minutes to sear well, then flip. After another 3 minutes your steak should be medium rare. Set aside.

Add your bell peppers and onion to the pan to deglaze, mixing occasionally. Cook until softened, about 10 minutes. Set aside.

CONTINUES

**PALEO BOWL,
CONTINUED**

Season your chicken heavily with the Creole
Seasoning. Heat the remaining 1 tablespoon of oil
in a medium pan over medium-high heat and sear
the chicken, 3 to 4 minutes on each side. Transfer
the chicken to the oven to finish cooking, about
15 minutes.

Slice your steak and chicken.

Fill your bowls up by putting quinoa on the bottom,
followed by a layer of spring mix and pickled onions
on top of that. Mix the spring mix and pickled onions.
Add pockets of your steak, chicken, avocado, and
sautéed onions and peppers, then top with several
large spoonfuls of Chimichurri and a big zigzag squirt
of sriracha. Garnish with additional pockets of pickled
onion and serve.

POZOLE VERDE

Okaaaaay, a lot to say about this one. First off, thank you to Mexico for inventing it. It's possibly the best chicken soup in the world, so once again, you guys have dominated another category of food. Second, thank you to Matty Matheson for introducing me to this version of it. Third, and maybe most important, there's no hominy in this, so it's technically not actually pozole. I've tried my hardest to enjoy hominy, and for some reason it just won't click. Instead, we're goin' Tex Mex style with some fried tortilla crisps. To those who stick up for traditional pozole, I have the utmost respect for tradition, and I promise, if we have the opportunity to cook and eat together, we'll make it the right way.

1	whole (4-pound) chicken, cut into 8 pieces
1	tablespoon kosher salt, plus more for seasoning
1	tablespoon freshly ground pepper, plus more for seasoning
¾	cup vegetable oil, divided
1	of every pepper you can find at the store (poblano, jalapeño, bell pepper, cubanelle, banana pepper, habanero, etc.), shoot for like 10 peppers total, all roughly chopped
1	white onion, quartered, plus ½ white onion, diced, divided
3	celery stalks, roughly chopped
2	carrots, peeled and roughly chopped
1	garlic bulb, cloves peeled and smashed
10	tomatillos, husks removed, washed, and halved
12	cups low-sodium chicken stock
4	(6-inch) corn tortillas, cut into strips
1	fresh jalapeño, thinly sliced
1	cup packed roughly chopped fresh cilantro
1	avocado, pitted, peeled, and thinly sliced, for garnish
	Sour cream, for garnish
1	fresh lime, cut into wedges, for serving

Season the chicken with salt and pepper. Heat ½ cup of the oil in a Dutch oven over medium heat. Sear the chicken pieces on all sides, 8 to 10 minutes, then remove them from the heat.

Working in batches in a food processor or blender, blend the peppers, the quartered onion, the celery, carrots, and garlic until they reach a mushy, uniform consistency. Add the mixture to the still-hot Dutch oven over medium heat and use it to deglaze the fond. Season with 1 tablespoon salt and pepper and reduce for at least 30 minutes to an hour, stirring frequently.

While your sofrito is cooking, spread the tomatillos out on a lightly oiled sheet pan and broil them until they're charred and cooked through, about 10 minutes, flipping them halfway through. Add the tomatillos to the sofrito mixture. Keep cooking it all down until it's been at least 30 minutes since the sofrito started cooking, then add your stock, raise the heat, and bring to a boil. Add your chicken back in, partially cover with a lid, and cook for another 3 hours. Taste for seasoning; it'll probably need another big pinch of salt.

CONTINUES

Fill the bottom of a medium skillet with the remaining vegetable oil over medium-high heat. Add the tortilla strips and shallow-fry them until crispy, about 5 minutes or until golden brown.

Once your soup has cooked down, it's ready to plate. Have your mise ready on the side, so guests can customize each of their bowls with tortilla strips, jalapeño, the diced onion, cilantro, avocado, sour cream, and lime wedges.

Plate and enjoy!

QUESO GORDITA CRUNCH

I have the utmost respect for Taco Bell. Whoever develops their recipes deserves some type of fast-food award. They are my go-to late night Postmates order, and it hits every single time, usually. Had to pay homage here. As much as I love Taco Bell, this homemade version is obviously like fifteen times as good.

1 tablespoon extra-virgin olive oil

1 white onion, finely diced, divided

2 tablespoons tomato paste

1 tablespoon garlic powder

1 tablespoon onion powder

1 teaspoon paprika

1 teaspoon cayenne

1 teaspoon chili powder

1 teaspoon cumin

1 teaspoon kosher salt, plus more for seasoning

1 teaspoon freshly ground black pepper

1 pound 80/20 ground beef

2 cups beef stock

2 cups vegetable oil

6 medium flour tortillas

   Cheese Sauce (Queso) (page 111)

   Fire Sauce (page 102)

   Shredded iceberg lettuce, for garnish

   Diced tomatoes, for garnish

   Chipotle Crema (page 102)

In a large pan over medium heat, heat the olive oil. Add half of the diced white onion to the pan, then add the tomato paste, garlic powder, onion powder, paprika, cayenne, chili powder, cumin, salt, and pepper and cook, stirring constantly for 1 to 2 minutes, then add the ground beef. Raise the heat to medium-high and cook, breaking the beef up as finely as you can, until browned, about 7 minutes. Reduce the heat to medium-low and add the beef stock. Continue to break everything up as much as possible and let your beef stock reduce to a chili-like consistency, 10 to 15 minutes. Set aside.

Pour the vegetable oil into a medium skillet over medium heat. One at a time, fry 3 of the tortillas submerged in the oil until they begin to crisp, about 10 seconds. Then flip the tortilla and bend it in half using a fork or tongs. Allow the tortilla to cook in this shape for 10 to 15 more seconds on each side, or until the tortilla is crisped to your liking, spooning the hot oil into the middle of the folded tortilla to crisp the center. Remove each tortilla from the oil and set it aside on a paper towel–lined plate.

Place an unfried tortilla flat on a plate. Spread some Queso over the tortilla. Place the fried tortilla in the middle. Spoon beef into the fried tortilla, top that with Fire Sauce, garnish with lettuce and tomato, then drizzle with Chipotle Crema. To serve and eat, wrap the unfried tortilla up around the fried one.

FIRE SAUCE

½ cup minced pickled jalapeños
3 tablespoons tomato paste
½ tablespoon cayenne
½ tablespoon onion powder
½ tablespoon garlic powder
½ tablespoon chili powder
½ tablespoon paprika
½ tablespoon kosher salt
½ tablespoon freshly ground black pepper

In a medium saucepan over medium-low heat, stir together 2 cups water with the jalapeños, tomato paste, cayenne, onion powder, garlic powder, chili powder, paprika, salt, and pepper. Simmer for 8 minutes, allow to cool for 10 minutes, then transfer the mixture to a blender and blend until smooth.

MAKES: ABOUT 1½ CUPS

CHIPOTLE CREMA

Going to leave the measurements out of this crema sauce so you can practice intuitive cooking. Also, I forgot them.

Chipotle in adobo
Sour cream
Juice of 3 fresh limes
Fresh cilantro
Kosher salt

Put the chipotle, sour cream, lime juice, and cilantro into a blender and blend until smooth. Season with salt.

MAKES: 1 TO 2 CUPS

CHICKEN TAQUITOS WITH CHARRED TOMATILLO SALSA

I know that no matter what I call these, a lot of you are going to passionately disagree with me on the name. The debate between calling these flautas, tacos dorados, and taquitos is one of the most heated arguments I've ever seen in my comments section. I learned how to make them from a phenomenal chef named Magdalena and she calls them taquitos, so I'm going to stick with that, but if you call them something different, I apologize. Hopefully when you try them, you'll forgive me.

2   large boneless, skinless chicken breasts

2   boneless, skinless chicken thighs

¼   teaspoon kosher salt, plus more for seasoning

¼   teaspoon freshly ground black pepper, plus more for seasoning

½   teaspoon garlic powder

½   teaspoon chili powder

6   tablespoons vegetable oil, divided

1   recipe Charred Tomatillo Salsa (page 172), divided

12 (6-inch) yellow corn tortillas (Mission brand if possible)

2   avocados, pitted and peeled

2   garlic cloves, minced

    Mexican crema, for garnish

    Cotija cheese, for garnish

    Sprigs of fresh cilantro, for garnish

    Juice of 1 fresh lime

Season your chicken breasts and thighs with the salt, pepper, garlic powder, and chili powder. Heat 1 tablespoon of the oil in a large pan over medium heat and add your chicken. Sear on both sides until cooked through, about 8 minutes per side. Shred the chicken with two forks and add half of your tomatillo salsa to the pan with the chicken. Mix the shredded chicken and salsa and cook, stirring occasionally, until the chicken is well saturated with salsa, about 2 minutes. Set aside.

Fill the bottom of a large pan with the remaining oil and bring to medium heat. In a damp paper towel, microwave your tortillas for 30 seconds or until warmed through. Place about 3 tablespoons of chicken in each tortilla and roll up your taquitos. Carefully lay them seam side down in the hot oil. If you're having trouble keeping them together, use toothpicks. Fry on all sides until deeply golden brown and crunchy, 2 to 3 minutes.

Dice the avocados and add them to your remaining green salsa. Add the minced garlic, a pinch more of salt and pepper, and mix together.

Top your taquitos with your salsa, crema, cotija cheese, a few sprigs of cilantro, and lime juice and serve.

TACOS IN A BAG OR WALKING TACOS

This is the perfect junk food meal for anyone between the ages of four and ninety. It hits particularly differently if you're drunk or high. I've heard. It's an endlessly customizable bag of cheesy, meaty, acidic, crunchy slop. This is also one of the most amazing novelty party meals ever invented. Each person can pick their favorite bag of chips and apply any number of toppings.

(For reference—Hank's bag is Flaming Hot Cheetos, topped with nacho cheese, sour cream, taco meat, guacamole, pico, pickled jalapeños, and lime.)

1 **tablespoon extra-virgin olive oil**

1 **white onion, finely diced, divided**

2 **tablespoons tomato paste**

1 **tablespoon garlic powder**

1 **tablespoon onion powder**

1 **teaspoon paprika**

1 **teaspoon cayenne, plus more for garnish, optional**

1 **teaspoon chili powder**

1 **teaspoon cumin**

1 **teaspoon kosher salt, plus more for seasoning**

1 **teaspoon freshly ground black pepper**

1 **pound 80/20 ground beef**

2 **cups beef stock**

3 **vine-ripe tomatoes, diced**

2 **fresh jalapeños, minced**

4 **garlic cloves, finely minced, divided**

2 **fresh limes**

3 **avocados, pitted, peeled, and scooped**

1 **fresh lemon**

A wide variety of personal bags of chips, common options are Fritos, Frito BBQ Twists, Doritos, and Hot Cheetos

Cheese Sauce (Queso; page 111)

Sour cream, for garnish

Pickled jalapeños, for garnish

Fresh cilantro, optional, for garnish

In a large pan over medium heat, heat the olive oil. Add half of your diced white onion to the pan, then add the tomato paste, garlic powder, onion powder, paprika, cayenne, chili powder, cumin, salt, and pepper and cook, stirring constantly, for 1 to 2 minutes, then add your ground beef. Raise the heat to medium-high and cook, breaking the beef up as finely as you can, until browned, about 7 minutes. Reduce the heat to medium-low and add your stock. Continue to break everything up as much as possible and let your stock reduce to a chili-like consistency, 10 to 15 minutes.

Mix your fresh, diced tomatoes with your remaining diced onion, the jalapeño, and 2 cloves of the minced garlic. Add a squirt of lime and a large pinch of salt and mash everything around to mix.

Mash your avocados with the remaining cloves of minced garlic, a large squeeze of lemon, and a big pinch of salt.

Cut your bag of chips open with scissors lengthwise, then add your Cheese Sauce, taco meat, sour cream, guacamole, pico, a few pickled jalapeños, and a squirt of lime. Garnish with a dusting of cayenne and some cilantro, if desired. Enjoy with a plastic fork.

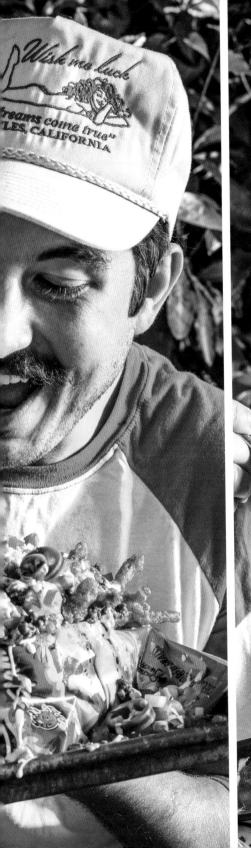

CHEESE SAUCE (QUESO)

1 pound American cheese, cubed

1 cup whole milk

1 (8-ounce) can diced tomatoes

2 cups sliced pickled jalapeños, divided

½ cup pickled jalapeño brine

1 tablespoon garlic powder

1 tablespoon onion powder

1 teaspoon paprika

1 teaspoon cayenne

½ tablespoon kosher salt

In a saucepan over medium-low heat, combine the cheese, milk, tomatoes, 1 cup of the diced pickled jalapeños, the jalapeño brine, your garlic powder, onion powder, paprika, cayenne, and salt. Stir constantly until it melts into a perfect queso, 10 to 15 minutes. Keep over low heat until serving. Garnish with the remaining sliced jalapeños.

MAKES: 3 CUPS
PREP TIME: 5 MIN
COOK TIME: 15 MIN
TOTAL TIME: 20 MIN

BANG BANG SHRIMP TACOS

This is kind of a stunt food taco, but it's one of the most delicious things in this book. You also don't need to serve these in a taco—Bang Bang Shrimp Tempura is perfect as an appetizer garnished with some green onions.

5	fresh serrano peppers
1	cup apple cider vinegar
2	teaspoons kosher salt, divided, plus more for seasoning
4	cups vegetable oil
2	cups all-purpose flour
3	large eggs, whisked with a splash of water
3	cups panko
3	tablespoons Cajun seasoning
1	pound peeled and deveined medium-size shrimp
12	(6-inch) street taco–style corn tortillas
½	cup sweet chili sauce
½	cup sriracha
½	cup Hellmann's or Best Foods mayonnaise
	Juice of 1 fresh lime
	Caramelized Onions (page 177), for garnish
	Fresh cilantro leaves, for garnish

Using a mandoline on setting #3, thinly slice your serrano peppers. Put them in a medium bowl with your vinegar and 1 teaspoon of salt. Make sure the peppers are submerged so that they will become lightly pickled, and set them aside for later.

In a large pot, heat the vegetable oil over medium heat to 350°F.

Place your flour, egg wash, and panko in separate shallow bowls for dredging. Season the panko with Cajun seasoning. Dredge the shrimp in the flour, then the egg wash, then the panko. Working in batches, carefully add the shrimp to the oil and fry them, until the panko is golden brown, 3 to 4 minutes. Remove to a paper towel–lined plate and immediately season with salt.

Carefully add the corn tortillas to the oil and quickly fry them for 15 to 30 seconds.

In a large mixing bowl, mix the sweet chili sauce, sriracha, mayo, lime juice, and the remaining 1 teaspoon of salt. Toss your fried shrimp in the Bang Bang sauce.

Remove the tails from the shrimp and add two shrimps per tortilla, with a hefty spoonful of Caramelized Onions, a couple quick pickled serrano peppers, and whole cilantro leaves to garnish. Serve immediately.

CALIFORNIA BURRITO

First, I should explain what this is: Essentially, someone in San Diego took a burrito and put French fries in it. The important difference here is that the French fries replace the beans and rice as the main carb; however, San Diegans will fight tooth and nail over the different/correct ways to make these burritos. This is another recipe that inevitably causes explosive arguments in the comments section. There is some pretty blatant irony in getting mad at someone for making an already derivative recipe differently than you do, but I digress. Made correctly, this burrito is a work of art. Our main priority is going to be making sure the French fries are crispy enough to withstand the onslaught of wet, juicy ingredients in the burrito, so these need to be the crunchiest, airiest French fries of all time. For this burrito, we'll have fries, carne asada, pico, guac, sour cream, fresh green salsa, pickled jalapeños, and shredded cheese.

1	**pound skirt steak**
	Carne Asada marinade (page 89)

PICO

1	**cup diced tomato**
⅔	**cup diced red onion**
½	**cup seeded and diced fresh jalapeños**
1	**teaspoon kosher salt**
	Juice of 1 fresh lime

3	**XL flour tortillas from a Mexican restaurant or Mexican market (the store-bought tortillas in a zip bag typically won't be big enough and they aren't as good)**
	Sour cream
	Guacamole (page 175)
	Fresh Green Salsa (page 173)
	French Fries (page 66)
	Quick Pickled Jalapeños (page 197)
1½	**cups shredded Monterey Jack cheese**
2	**tablespoons extra-virgin olive oil**

In a nonreactive bowl or dish, marinate your steak in the Carne Asada marinade. Ensure that the steak is fully submerged so that the marinade is in contact with all sides of it. Marinate for 2 to 3 hours.

MAKE THE PICO: In a medium bowl, mix together the tomato, onion, jalapeños, salt, and lime juice. Set aside in the refrigerator.

Heat a cast iron skillet over high heat for at least 5 minutes. Once it's ripping hot, pull the steak from the marinade and add it directly to the pan. Press the steak down to ensure full surface coverage and sear for 2 to 3 minutes per side for medium rare. The steak will smoke a lot and burn a little bit; that's fine. If you want to deglaze your pan between batches, add a bit of water and scrape the bottom with a spatula. Let the steak rest on a plate to retain the excess juice that comes out. Cube your steak up into ½-inch chunks, then mix it with the excess steak juice.

CONTINUES

TO BUILD YOUR BURRITO: In the center of the tortilla place the sour cream, guacamole, steak, pico, green salsa, French fries, and pickled jalapeños. Sprinkle a handful of shredded cheese all over the filling and the surrounding tortilla. Fold the bottom of the tortilla over the filling, then tuck it under. Fold the sides in so they're creased all the way to the top of the tortilla and then roll it up. Heat the oil in a large skillet over medium heat. Sear the burrito crease side down until the cheese is melted, 1 to 2 minutes. Flip and sear the other side.

Enjoy! Sorry that took so long!

STEAK AND SCALLOPS WITH ITALIAN SALSA VERDE

We gettin' fancy with this one. I know I could've called it surf and turf, but Steak and Scallops sounds much cooler in my humble opinion. Make sure your scallops are nice and fresh, by the way, yet another reason to cultivate that good fishmonger relationship. Without further ado, I present the fanciest meal in this book.

FOR THE ITALIAN SALSA VERDE

- 3 **garlic cloves**
- 1 **teaspoon flaky salt**
- 1 **cup packed chopped fresh parsley leaves**
- ½ **cup chopped fresh mint leaves**
- 3 **tablespoons minced, drained capers**
- 1 **medium-size shallot, minced**
- 3 **anchovies**
- 1 **teaspoon chili flakes**
- 3 **tablespoons extra-virgin olive oil**
  Juice of ½ fresh lemon

FOR THE SCALLOPS

- 1 **pound sea scallops**
- 2 **teaspoons kosher salt**
- 2 **teaspoons freshly ground black pepper**
- ½ **cup vegetable oil**
- 3 **tablespoons unsalted butter**

FOR THE FILET

- 2 **large (7-ounce) filet mignons**
- 2 **teaspoons flaky salt, plus more for garnish**
- 2 **teaspoons coarsely ground black pepper**
  Vegetable oil
- 6 **tablespoons unsalted butter**
- 1 **bulb of garlic, cut in half**
- 3 **fresh rosemary sprigs**
- 3 **fresh thyme sprigs**
- 6 **fresh sage leaves**

Flaky salt, for garnish

MAKE THE ITALIAN SALSA VERDE: Put the garlic and flaky salt into a mortar and pestle and grind to a paste. Add the parsley, mint, capers, shallot, anchovies, and chili flakes and grind until the sauce reaches a rustic salsa consistency. Add the olive oil and lemon juice and grind everything together for an additional minute or so, making sure to crush any large chunks. Set aside.

MAKE THE SCALLOPS: Pat your scallops dry and season flat sides with the salt and pepper. Fill the bottom of a large pan with ¼ inch of oil and bring up to high heat. Gently lay your scallops in the oil and sear them, 1 to 2 minutes. Flip them and add the butter. Baste the scallops with the butter and oil and cook until a dark brown crust has formed, another 1 to 2 minutes, then remove them from the pan and set aside.

MAKE THE FILETS: Season your filets heavily on all sides with flaky salt and pepper.

Fill the bottom of a large skillet with a ¼ inch of vegetable oil and heat over medium-high heat. Once the oil starts to smoke, add your filets. The bottom of the filet should be submerged in a ¼ inch of oil to ensure a good crust. Sear for 3 minutes, moving your steak around the pan midway through. Once the crust reaches a deep golden brown, flip and sear for another minute.

CONTINUES

Remove the steaks from the pan and pour the excess oil into a bowl to discard once cooled. Add the butter, garlic, rosemary, thyme, and sage, and place your steaks back in the pan. Baste them liberally for about 2 minutes.

Plate by slicing your filet in ½-inch slices and fanning them out. Add your scallops on top of that and drizzle salsa verde all over everything. Finish with a big pinch of flaky salt and enjoy.

PRIME RIB ROAST

This one's a showstopper and relatively easy to make. But I'd highly recommend a meat thermometer. I've fucked this one up a couple times trying to cook it off instinct alone, and it's been heartbreaking. However, if you have a meat probe, you should be golden, and when you finally achieve that perfect cross-section in front of all your family and friends, and everyone goes "WOOOWWW," it's an indescribably awesome feeling. If you want a nice little gravy for the side, add some beef bouillon and cornstarch to a pot of beef stock and cook it down until it's nice and thick.

FOR THE COMPOUND BUTTER

- 1   cup fresh rosemary leaves
- 1   cup fresh thyme sprigs
- 1   cup fresh oregano leaves
- 1   cup fresh sage leaves, roughly chopped
- 2   garlic bulbs, cloves peeled
- ½   cup (1 stick) unsalted butter
- 1   tablespoon Dijon mustard

FOR THE ROAST

-     4-bone prime rib roast
- 1   tablespoon flaky salt
- 2   tablespoons freshly ground black pepper, divided
- 2   tablespoons unsalted butter
- 1   tablespoon extra-virgin olive oil
- 3   large carrots, peeled and thinly sliced
- 3   celery stalks, thinly sliced
- 2   red onions, thinly sliced
- 1   tablespoon beef bouillon base
- 1   tablespoon kosher salt
- 8   cups beef stock
- 1   cup Worcestershire sauce
- 1   cup thinly sliced fresh chives, for garnish

Preheat the oven to 325°F.

MAKE THE COMPOUND BUTTER: In a blender, place the rosemary, thyme, oregano, and sage. Add the garlic cloves and blend to mince. Add the butter cut into cubes and the Dijon mustard. Blend until the butter reaches a soft, whipped consistency and everything is combined.

MAKE THE ROAST: Slather the entire roast with your compound butter and place rib side down on a sheet pan fitted with a wire rack. Season heavily on all sides with the flaky salt and 1 tablespoon of the pepper.

Roast about 1½ hours or until the internal temperature of meat reaches 130°F. Timing may vary, so be sure to check the temperature periodically. Remove the meat from the pan and allow it to rest for 30 minutes.

In a large pot, heat the butter and the oil over medium heat. Stir in the carrots, celery, and onions, then add the beef bouillon, kosher salt, and the remaining 1 tablespoon of pepper. Cook, stirring, for about 30 minutes, then add your beef stock and Worcestershire sauce. Bring to a simmer and cook until reduced by about 40 percent, about 45 minutes. Strain the gravy through a fine-mesh sieve, using a large spoon to push all the liquid out of your solids.

Slice your prime rib and serve with the gravy. Garnish with the chives.

TRI TIP

Tri tip is objectively the most flavorful cut of beef. That's not statistically proven or anything, but maybe it should be. The reason I wanted to include this recipe is to show that you don't need a BBQ or smoker to make the perfect tri tip. It's mostly the rosemary garlic butter basting situation that makes it so good, and basting on a BBQ just doesn't hit the same in my opinion. Apologies if I've offended any pitmasters out there but you know it's true.

1 large tri tip, 2⅓ to 3 pounds
3 tablespoons vegetable oil, divided
2 tablespoons kosher salt
2 tablespoons freshly ground black pepper
2 tablespoons garlic powder
½ cup (1 stick) unsalted butter, cubed
6 crushed garlic cloves
3 sprigs fresh rosemary
3 sprigs fresh thyme
   Chimichurri (page 163), for serving

Preheat oven to 300°F.

Place the tri tip on a sheet pan and slather on 2 tablespoons of the oil. Season very heavily with the salt, pepper, and garlic powder. Massage the seasoning into the meat with your hands.

Transfer it to a wire rack–lined sheet pan and place it in the oven. Cook 30 minutes to 1 hour, until the internal temp reaches 130°F, checking as the time does vary between tri tips. Remove and let rest for 10 minutes on a wire rack.

While it's resting, heat a large pan over high heat. Put the remaining 1 tablespoon of oil in the pan, then add your steak, followed by the butter, garlic, rosemary, and thyme. Baste the meat with a large metal spoon and let the butter and oil sear the sides of the steak that aren't making contact with the pan. Flip once a solid sear is achieved, about 2 minutes, and repeat the basting and searing process. Transfer after 2 minutes to a cutting board and let rest for 10 minutes.

Slice and serve with Chimichurri.

TRI TIP, PAGE 122

SERVES: 4   PREP TIME: 20 MIN   COOK TIME:
2 HRS 30 MIN   TOTAL TIME:
2 HRS 50 MIN

BAKED RIBS

I made these for the first time because I was supposed to be making a fancy version of a McRib sandwich, but I ended up eating all the ribs before I could put them on the sandwich. It blew my mind how fantastic they turned out and how easy they were to make. It's also a great reason to make BBQ sauce, which I always think has a lot of mystery behind it. In reality, it's literally just ketchup mixed with sugar, spices, and vinegar. This recipe includes a pretty basic BBQ sauce, but you can add a different citrus, more mustard, or even replace the ketchup with mayonnaise and make an Alabama white sauce.

2	racks baby back ribs
½	cup yellow mustard
2	tablespoons garlic powder
2	tablespoons onion powder
2	tablespoons kosher salt
2	tablespoons freshly ground black pepper
1	tablespoon paprika
1	tablespoon cayenne
1	tablespoon harissa powder
1	cup apple cider vinegar, divided
2	cups ketchup
⅔	cup light brown sugar
2	tablespoons whole grain mustard
	Juice of 1 fresh lemon

Preheat your oven to 300°F.

Remove the membrane from the back of your ribs (you can ask your butcher to do this). Pat them dry with a paper towel, then brush a layer of yellow mustard on them as a binder.

In a medium bowl, whisk together the garlic powder, onion powder, salt, pepper, paprika, cayenne, and harissa powder. Reserve half of the spice mixture and sprinkle the other half all over your ribs. Place them bone side down on a couple of large sheets of foil and pour a couple of tablespoons of vinegar underneath each of the ribs. Double-wrap them in foil and put them in the oven on a sheet pan.

In a large saucepan over medium-low heat, combine your ketchup, brown sugar, remaining spice blend, remaining vinegar, whole grain mustard, and lemon juice. Bring to a low simmer and cook, stirring frequently, until thickened, about 10 minutes. Remove from the heat.

Remove your ribs from the oven. Crank the heat to 450°F.

Open up the foil and brush the ribs generously with your BBQ sauce. Return them to the oven and allow them to glaze, about 20 minutes, then pull them. The meat should pull off the bone pretty easily but still have some bite to it. Cut your ribs up and serve with the remaining BBQ sauce.

BRUSCHETTA BRICK CHICKEN

I learned how to make bruschetta from my mom, who is a salt and garlic fanatic. For that reason, I'm going to write this recipe with her in mind and use a lot more salt and garlic than might typically be included. Feel free to follow these instructions exactly for an extra flavorful sauce or reduce the salt and garlic for a milder *cough, worse* version.

2   **skin-on, bone-in chicken legs**
½   **teaspoon kosher salt**
1   **tablespoon vegetable oil**
1   **loaf crusty sourdough baguette**
1   **recipe Classic Bruschetta (page 131)**

Remove the chicken from the refrigerator 1 to 2 hours before cooking. Pat dry, then season with the salt. In a large pan, heat the oil over medium heat. Lay the chicken skin side down in the oil. Press down with your hand to make sure the full surface area of the chicken is touching the pan, then place your brick or cast iron pan (or any other heavy flat object you can find) on top of your chicken. This should be heavy enough to flatten out both legs pretty significantly. If you use an actual brick and it's not covering both thighs, put a pan over them first and then put the brick on the pan. The chicken should be gently, softly sizzling.

After 8 minutes, check the skin of your chicken. It should be reaching a deep golden brown and the meat should be almost cooked through. If everything looks good and like it's not about to burn, keep cooking the same way until the meat reaches an internal temperature of 165°F, another 5 to 7 minutes. The skin should be crispy like glass and perfectly golden brown edge to edge. Remove the chicken from the pan and set it aside to rest, skin side up.

Cut slices of the bread on the diagonal and fry them in the rendered chicken fat until crispy, 4 to 5 minutes.

Put a couple of spoonfuls of the bruschetta mixture on each plate, then place the chicken legs on top, skin side up. Add a couple of pieces of crostini to each plate and spoon more bruschetta on top of the chicken. Enjoy!

CLASSIC BRUSCHETTA

3 cups thinly sliced organic cherry tomatoes
1 cup packed chiffonade fresh basil leaves
1 cup extra-virgin olive oil
5 garlic cloves, minced
1 tablespoon kosher salt
Crostini, for serving

Mix your tomatoes, basil, olive oil, garlic, and salt in a bowl. Using a wood spoon or spatula, smush everything around for a minute to slightly break the tomatoes up.

Serve with crostini.

SERVES: 2
PREP TIME: 10 MIN
COOK TIME: N/A
TOTAL TIME: 10 MIN

ROAST CHICKEN AND GARLIC BREAD

This is the first real recipe I ever learned how to cook. It's something my mom made at least once a week when I was growing up, and it's still my all-time favorite comfort food. It's also probably the easiest main course in this book. The final plate includes: perfect roast chicken, roast veggies, amazing broth, garlic bread, and a simple green salad.

6	large, peeled carrots
3	celery stalks
½	pound fingerling potatoes
2⅓	yellow onions, divided
1	garlic bulb plus 6 peeled cloves, divided
2	tablespoons extra-virgin olive oil, divided
3	tablespoons kosher salt, divided
2	tablespoons freshly ground black pepper
1	(4-pound) chicken
½	fresh lemon
3	sprigs fresh thyme
3	cups chicken stock
½	bunch fresh parsley
½	cup (1 stick) unsalted butter
1	rustic Italian or sourdough baguette
2	cups each red leaf lettuce, butter lettuce, and green leaf lettuce
⅓	cup Balsamic Dressing (page 157)

Preheat the oven to 425°F.

Start by very roughly chopping your carrots, celery, potatoes, and 2 of your onions. This doesn't need to look sexy—just aim for around 2 inches per chunk. Cut the garlic bulb in half. Lay everything down in a large roasting dish and slather with 1 tablespoon of the olive oil. Season with salt and pepper and shake everything around.

Place your chicken breast side up on top of your vegetables. Stuff with the remaining third of an onion, the lemon, and the thyme. Slather generously with the remaining olive oil, then season with kosher salt. The method of seasoning the chicken is relatively important—take almost a small handful of salt, and slowly sprinkle it from high above so the falling salt spreads out and evenly covers the surface of the chicken. Once you've fully covered the exposed parts of the chicken, move around the wings and drums to season underneath and the more hidden areas. You can season the cavity if you want, but I'm pretty sure it doesn't do anything. Add the chicken stock to the bottom of your roasting dish and place it in the oven. Roast for about 1 hour, or until the internal temp reaches 165°F.

CONTINUES

While the chicken is cooking, put the garlic cloves, the leaves of the parsley, 1 tablespoon of salt, and the butter, cut into quarters, into your food processor and blend until the mixture reaches a soft whipped consistency. Cut the baguette in half lengthwise and slather your garlic butter on both sides.

Once the chicken is done, remove it to let it rest and add the garlic bread to the oven. Remove when the butter is melted and the bread is golden brown, 7 to 10 minutes.

In a salad bowl, mix your spring mix with the Balsamic Dressing.

Carve the chicken and plate with salad, veggies, and garlic bread, spooning heavy amounts of the juices from the bottom of the roasting dish onto your plate. This broth is incredibly flavorful and amazing when mopped up with the garlic bread. If I were you, I'd make a perfect little chicken sandwich with broth-soaked garlic bread, chicken, salad, and your roasted onions.

RACK OF LAMB WITH RED WINE REDUCTION SAUCE, GLAZED CARROTS, AND GARLIC BREAD

If you're ever feeling insecure, make this for someone. Make it for a significant other, a friend, your parents, or literally anyone else, and I guarantee they will be like, how the fuck did you do that? And you'll immediately feel better. In my opinion, it's the most impressive thing you can make while expending the least amount of energy. It's tough to screw up, but it looks like a Michelin-star meal.

¼	cup plus 2 tablespoons extra-virgin olive oil, divided
2	garlic bulbs, peeled and thinly sliced, plus 13 peeled cloves, divided
3	shallots, finely minced
	Pinch kosher salt, plus more for seasoning
	Pinch freshly ground black pepper, plus more for seasoning
1	bottle of pretty good red wine; dry cabernet works well
8	cups beef stock
4	tablespoons cornstarch
1¼	cups (2½ sticks) cold unsalted butter, divided
½	tablespoon beef bouillon base
1	(8-bone) rack of lamb
¼	cup vegetable oil, divided
2	bunches multicolored carrots with greens still attached
2	tablespoons Balsamic Dressing (page 157)
1	tablespoon honey
½	cup fresh rosemary sprigs
½	cup fresh thyme sprigs
½	cup fresh sage leaves
½	cup fresh oregano
1½	tablespoons Dijon mustard
1	loaf crusty Italian or sourdough baguette

Coat the bottom of a large pot with ¼ cup of the olive oil over medium-low heat. Add the two sliced garlic bulbs and your shallots and season with a big pinch of salt and pepper. Cook, stirring, until you start to notice some color, about 2 minutes, then add a little over half of your wine. Raise the heat to medium and bring to a simmer. Reduce until almost all the liquid is gone, 10 to 15 minutes, then add the beef stock and reduce for another 15 minutes. In a medium bowl, whisk the cornstarch with 1 cup of water, then whisk it into your sauce. Next whisk in 3 tablespoons of the butter and the bouillon. Whisk until the sauce reaches desired thickness. Taste the sauce and add additional salt and pepper, if you think it needs it. The sauce should be pretty savory and have a kick of pepper. Strain through a fine-mesh sieve and reserve.

Coat your rack of lamb with 2 tablespoons of the vegetable oil, then heavily season with salt and pepper. Heat 2 tablespoons of vegetable oil in a large skillet over medium-high heat, and sear the lamb on all sides. Remove to a roasting dish to let cool.

CONTINUES

Preheat the oven to 425°F.

Cut the green tops off your carrots and reserve. Wash your carrots of any dirt and dry off. Put them in a roasting dish and toss with 2 tablespoons of the olive oil, salt, and pepper. Roast for about 20 minutes, or until the thick part of the carrot is knife-tender.

While the carrots are roasting, microwave 4 tablespoons (½ stick) of the butter with the Balsamic Dressing, honey, and 5 garlic cloves, minced, 1 to 2 minutes, or until melted. Pour this mixture over your carrots and mix them around with the glaze. Place the carrots back in the oven and roast until they begin to caramelize and char, 5 to 10 minutes more. Remove, then garnish by sprinkling with a small handful of roughly chopped carrot tops.

FOR THE COMPOUND BUTTER: In a food processor, blend the rosemary, thyme, sage, and oregano together with the remaining garlic cloves. Add the Dijon mustard and ¾ cup (1½ sticks) of butter. Blend until the butter reaches a soft, whipped consistency, then slather all over your rack of lamb. Roast for 20 to 25 minutes, or until the lamb reaches an internal temperature of 130°F according to a meat thermometer.

Use any leftover compound butter to slather on the baguette. Season it heavily with salt and pepper, and bake at 425°F until crispy, 10 to 15 minutes. Plate the lamb up with the sauce, carrots, and bread.

RACK OF LAMB WITH RED WINE REDUCTION SAUCE, GLAZED CARROTS, AND GARLIC BREAD, CONTINUED

DUCK BREAST WITH POTATO CHIPS AND PAN SAUCE

Duck breast is another cut of meat that I think is often overlooked. It's easy to prepare and maybe better than steak. It's red meat, so you can cook it medium rare, but it's also a bird, so there is a thick layer of delicious fatty skin attached. It's like all the good parts of a steak combined with all the good parts of chicken, and arguably easier to master than both. This method of cooking essentially has a built-in self-timer. More and more duck fat will render out into the pan as you cook, allowing you to gauge the doneness based on how much fat has built up. Once you have a hefty pool of fat and have been basting your duck for five or so minutes, you can pull it off the heat.

2   large duck breasts
1   teaspoon kosher salt, divided
½   teaspoon freshly ground black pepper
2   sprigs fresh rosemary
3   garlic cloves, smashed
1   shallot, finely diced
1   cup red wine, dry cabernet works well
2   cups beef stock
2   tablespoons cold unsalted butter
3   tablespoons chopped fresh chives
    Potato Chips (recipe follows)

To prepare your duck, start by scoring the skin with a very sharp knife in a crosshatch pattern. Only slice through a bit of the first layer and avoid cutting into the meat. Pat the skin side dry and season with salt. Let the duck sit for 10 minutes and pat it dry again. Lay it skin side down in a cold pan, press down for full surface area coverage, and turn the flame on to medium heat. Season the other side with the remaining salt and the pepper. After a few minutes you should start to hear the skin sizzle and see some duck fat rendering into the pan. Once enough fat has rendered out to baste the duck, add the rosemary and garlic and start to baste. Baste on and off until medium rare, 5 to 6 minutes. Your duck meat should have some give but also spring back a small amount. At this point it's time to remove the duck and start the pan sauce.

Pour the excess duck fat into a bowl and reserve for something else. Set the rosemary sprigs aside. Discard the garlic. Add the shallot to your pan to deglaze, scraping all the crispy bits off the bottom of the pan. Cook, stirring constantly, until lightly browned, about 2 minutes, then add the wine. Reduce this mixture until there's almost no liquid left, about 4 minutes, then add the beef stock. Reduce by half, then whisk in the butter. Taste and adjust for seasoning.

POTATO CHIPS

I added an extra potato to the ingredients. Enjoy those extra chips before bed.

3 Yukon gold potatoes
3 tablespoons kosher salt
4 cups vegetable oil
1 tablespoon Old Bay seasoning
½ tablespoon onion powder

Slice the duck into 1-inch pieces and plate. Spoon your pan sauce over the duck and add a heavy sprinkle of chives and some of the fried rosemary leaves from your duck basting. Add a large handful of potato chips to the plate. Combining everything into one bite is the best way to eat this.

Using a mandoline on setting #2, slice your potatoes. Lay them flat on a paper towel, not overlapping, as you go. Pat them dry with another paper towel, then sprinkle the salt from high above to cover each slice of potato. Let them sit for 10 minutes to allow the salt to draw out moisture.

While you wait, in a large, deep skillet, heat your oil to 350°F.

After 10 minutes, wipe the salt and excess moisture off the potatoes with a paper towel. The drier you can get them the better. Carefully add the chips to the oil in batches and fry them until they are golden brown, about 8 minutes, then remove them to drain on paper towels. Immediately sprinkle them with the Old Bay and onion powder.

SERVES: 2 TO 3
PREP TIME: 15 MIN
COOK TIME: 24 MIN
TOTAL TIME: 39 MIN

DUCK BREAST WITH POTATO CHIPS AND PAN SAUCE, PAGE 138

SAUCES, DIPS, AND SALSAS

I COULD WRITE A MANIFESTO ON SAUCES, BUT I'll spare you the reading. Instead, here are some of my go-to ingredients that you can pretty much just mix with mayo to make an amazing sauce. Combine at least two or three of these for something special.

- Worcestershire sauce
- Horseradish
- Lemon, lime, or any citrus as well as the grated zest
- Fresh chives, mint, parsley, cilantro, dill
- Fresh minced garlic
- Parmesan
- Finely diced cucumber
- Finely diced shallot
- Minced ginger
- Calabrian chilis
- Vinegar or pickle brine
- Caramelized onions
- Seasonings

Try combining a mixture of all the above ingredients and taste it, then go to town with SALT and PEPPER, paprika, onion powder, cayenne, garlic powder, harissa powder, chili flakes, or anything else you can find in your pantry. Another little cheat code if your sauce is lacking flavor, mix in a little bouillon . . . it's the easiest way to make mediocre food taste great and I know it's a little frowned upon but whatever, it works the exact same as spending 20 hours boiling down a stock. No offense to the purists out there but I've done both plenty of times and straight up, bouillon wins every time.

For Salsa!

I've figured out at least like 4 or 5 variations of salsa. The easiest is to just throw your fresh ingredients (tomato, onion, garlic, cilantro, jalapeño) in the blender with a tablespoon of chicken bouillon powder and call it a day. If you want a deeper color and flavor, go find some dried ancho chilis. Toast those in a pan in some olive oil with whole garlic cloves, organic tomato, chilis and onion, and a big pinch of salt. Once the garlic starts to take on some real color, add a big splash of water and cover. Let everything steam for a while, then add everything to a food processor with some cilantro and BOUILLON AGAIN. Make sure to include allllllll the liquid that's collected at the bottom of the pan. This is by far the most flavorful part of the salsa. BTW, I don't care if bouillon is a cheat code. It works like a charm, and we aren't going to intentionally make things harder to make for the sake of operating like a Michelin restaurant. All my respect to those who go the extra mile and spend the extra time.

MAYONNAISE AND AIOLI

Once you have nailed the foundation for mayonnaise, the variety of aioli you can make is literally endless. Write this mayonnaise algorithm on your kitchen window, Zuckerberg style, and expand out from here:

2 egg yolks + 1 tablespoon vinegar + 1 cup vegetable oil (slowly blended in) = mayonnaise

This omits any type of seasonings or flavor, so I wouldn't recommend stopping there. If you want to make a basic delicious mayonnaise, blend up some salt and garlic with your eggs. If you want to make a fancy mayonnaise, add some lemon juice and Dijon mustard as well. Always add the oil last, after you've mixed/blended the other ingredients, and add it very slowly. When I say slowly, I mean a couple of drops, then a couple more drops, then a couple more, until you've gotten about a quarter of the way through your oil, and then you can start to speed it up.

From there, you can take your aioli game to the moon. Throw in whatever you can think of that might taste good: roasted peppers, fried rosemary, sun-dried tomatoes, raspberries, or literally anything else (within reason). I did a cranberry aioli for a Thanksgiving leftover sandwich last year and it was incredible. Fancy restaurants in Oaxaca use cricket (*chapulines*) aioli to garnish their tostadas. The options are limitless.

The only tricky part can be making sure the aioli doesn't break. The easiest way I have found to keep your mayo from breaking is using an immersion blender and a Mason jar just barely large enough to fit the blender stick. Add your eggs and other flavorful items to the bottom and your oil on top. Push the immersion blender all the way to the bottom and turn it on. It will blend the eggs with the other ingredients first, and slowly drag the oil down and emulsify it with everything else. After thirty seconds or so, your mayo should start to take form. Otherwise, slowly adding your oil to a food processor or slowly whisking your oil into a bowl should work fine too. Just make sure to blend or whisk your other loose ingredients for a second before adding your oil.

If your aioli breaks, you can usually fix it by adding some eggs to a clean jar or blender, and slowly blending/whisking in your broken aioli. It's kind of a touch-and-go process, and sometimes you might just need to start from scratch again, but it's a quick learning curve and shouldn't happen more than a couple times.

Here's a simple example to get you started:

CONTINUES

ROASTED RED PEPPER AIOLI

½ red bell pepper, core removed
1 teaspoon extra-virgin olive oil
2 teaspoons plus 1 pinch kosher salt, divided
Pinch freshly ground black pepper
2 large egg yolks
1 tablespoon whole grain mustard
1 tablespoon red apple cider vinegar
2 garlic cloves
1 cup vegetable oil

Preheat the oven to 400°F.

To roast the red pepper, rub it with the olive oil and season it with a pinch of salt and pepper. Put it on a sheet pan and roast for 15 to 20 minutes.

Put the roasted pepper, egg yolks, mustard, vinegar, garlic, and the remaining 2 teaspoons of salt in a food processor. Blend for 15 seconds, then very slowly drizzle your oil in droplet by droplet until you've gotten a quarter of the way through it. Continue to add your oil a little faster, checking to make sure the consistency of the mayo is thickening up. Store your aiolis and mayos in a sealed container in the refrigerator for up to 2 weeks.

This may seem like a lot, but aioli has become a key component to almost everything we eat, and once you've nailed the basics, it's one of the most exciting and fun ways to experiment with food.

MAKES: 1½ CUPS
PREP TIME: 5 MIN
COOK TIME: 20 MIN
TOTAL TIME: 25 MIN

CREOLE REMOULADE

This should be called Mike Tyson sauce, 'cause it packs a serious punch. Bad joke, but truly this is the most flavorful sauce in this book. I'm sure you can imagine the amount of zing just by looking at some of the ingredients. Capers, gherkins, Dijon, Tabasco, and horseradish on their own have some of the most concentrated amounts of flavor in the world of everyday ingredients. Combining them is like bringing together the Avengers of flavor. I'm making it sound overwhelming, but somehow it isn't. There is a creamy element in this sauce that balances out all that twang and everything comes together very nicely. We'll be using this on the hot cod sandwich later, but it's an amazing dipping sauce for fried foods or vegetables, it works perfectly to dress an egg or chicken salad, and obviously it's great on sandwiches and burgers—it's very versatile and very delicious.

1   cup Hellmann's or Best Foods mayonnaise
2   tablespoons Dijon mustard
2   tablespoons finely chopped fresh parsley
    Juice of ½ fresh lemon
1   tablespoon finely chopped, drained capers
1   tablespoon finely chopped gherkins
2   teaspoons Creole seasoning
2   teaspoons Tabasco
4   garlic cloves, minced
1   teaspoon prepared horseradish
¼   cup finely sliced fresh chives

In a medium bowl, stir together the mayonnaise, mustard, parsley, lemon juice, capers, gherkins, Creole seasoning, Tabasco, garlic, horseradish, and chives. Adjust the seasoning as needed. Store in a sealed container in the refrigerator for up to 2 weeks.

CALABRIAN CHILI GARLIC AIOLI

Here, I'm basically just taking my two favorite ingredients and turning them into mayo. It's really not that impressive of an idea, but the outcome is a different story entirely. Because they're now in a mayonnaise form, they can basically be applied to anything, even boring stuff. It's like a limitless pill for food. (Like that movie where Bradley Cooper is a dumb loser but then takes a pill that gives his brain superhuman intelligence.) If you have some loser-ass, lame, boring-ass Bradley Cooper food, apply this aioli to it and now you have a masterpiece. Oh, all you have is raw broccoli? Hold up, let me get my Calabrian Chili Garlic Aioli. You're welcome for the super broccoli. Ah shit guys, all I have in my fridge is one tomato and some toast and Doja Cat is coming over! *Your random homie* bro, slice up those tomatoes and let me take care of the rest. Everyone claps and starts weeping tears of joy over the Calabrian chili aioli tomato toast. These are real situations that will happen in your life if you make this aioli.

6	medium Calabrian chilis
2	garlic bulbs, roasted (see Note)
3	garlic cloves (raw!)
3	large egg yolks
3	teaspoons kosher salt
	Juice of ½ fresh lemon
1½	cups vegetable oil

Put the chilis, roasted garlic, raw garlic, yolks, salt, and lemon juice in a food processor and blend for 10 seconds. Add the oil in a thin stream, while the processor is running, until your aioli emulsifies. Store in a sealed container in the refrigerator for up to 2 weeks. (See page 146 on mayos and aiolis for further instructions.)

NOTE: To roast the garlic bulbs, wrap them in foil and roast in a 400°F oven for 1 hour. Squeeze the softened garlic cloves out of their skins when done.

HORSERADISH GARLIC MAYO

The title of this one could basically double as the headnote, or even the entire recipe. The name of the sauce contains, in fact, most of the ingredients in the recipe. We are roasting the garlic and adding some Worcestershire sauce and chives, so I'll admit it's elevated a little bit past the title ingredients. Fun fact, this is my all-time most used sandwich sauce. I used it first with the French Dip (page 231), and now I use it so much it's basically just called sandwich sauce in my brain. If you don't have the time to roast the garlic, just grate some fresh garlic in there instead; it'll be just as awesome, only different.

1	cup Hellmann's or Best Foods mayonnaise
2	garlic bulbs, roasted (see Note)
⅓	cup Worcestershire sauce
3	tablespoons finely sliced fresh chives
1	tablespoon prepared horseradish
2	teaspoons kosher salt
2	teaspoons freshly ground black pepper

In a medium bowl, stir together the mayonnaise, garlic, Worcestershire sauce, chives, horseradish, salt, and black pepper. Store in a sealed container in the refrigerator for up to 2 weeks.

NOTE: To roast the garlic bulbs, wrap them in foil and roast in a 400°F oven for 1 hour. Squeeze the softened garlic cloves out of their skins when done.

SPICY RANCH

Homemade ranch is something that is very close to my heart. I feel oddly protective of it because people love to take digs at ranch. The problem is I usually agree with them. Store-bought ranch is awful. It's bad enough that ranch has this badge of shame as an unsophisticated/crappy condiment. I'm not trying to write a ranch manifesto here, but homemade ranch may be one of the most versatile and gourmet-ish sauces out there.

1   cup sour cream
1   cup Hellmann's or Best Foods mayonnaise
⅓   cup buttermilk
4   tablespoons thinly sliced fresh chives
4   tablespoons roughly chopped fresh dill
4   tablespoons finely chopped fresh parsley
    Juice of ¼ fresh lemon
1   tablespoon white wine vinegar or any other vinegar
3   garlic cloves, finely minced
1   teaspoon garlic powder
1   teaspoon onion powder
1   teaspoon cayenne
1   teaspoon kosher salt
1   teaspoon freshly ground black pepper

In a medium bowl, stir together the sour cream, mayonnaise, buttermilk, chives, dill, parsley, lemon juice, vinegar, garlic, garlic powder, onion powder, cayenne, salt, and pepper. Store in a sealed container in the refrigerator for up to 2 weeks.

FERAL SAUCE

While this recipe is my favorite version of this type of sauce, found on so many fast-food burgers, at the end of the day it's really the names that set all these burger sauces apart. They're all just variations of one mother sauce, and as much as I don't want to admit it, that sauce is thousand island dressing. No matter what your favorite burger place names their special sauce, they're all just elevated versions of that same shitty salad dressing. Thousand island dressing is like Viagra. Viagra was a huge failure for its intended purpose of helping with heart disease but a gigantic success in another way. Thousand island's original purpose of dressing salads is a disaster, but it just happens to be great on burgers.

1   **white onion, finely diced**

2   **tablespoons unsalted butter**

2   **teaspoons plus 1 pinch kosher salt, divided**

2   **teaspoons plus 1 pinch freshly ground black pepper, divided**

2   **tablespoons plus a dash Worcestershire sauce, divided**

1   **cup Hellmann's or Best Foods mayonnaise**

½   **cup ketchup**

2   **tablespoons finely minced dill pickle**

2   **tablespoons thinly sliced fresh chives**
    A squeeze of fresh lemon juice

1   **teaspoon paprika**

To caramelize the onion, throw it into a medium pan over medium heat with the butter, a big pinch of salt and pepper, and a dash of Worcestershire sauce. Cook, stirring continuously, until browned, about 45 minutes. Remove the onions and refrigerate for 15 minutes to cool.

In a medium bowl, stir together the caramelized onion, the mayonnaise, ketchup, pickle, chives, the remaining 2 tablespoons of Worcestershire sauce, the lemon juice, paprika, and the remaining 2 teaspoons salt and 2 teaspoons pepper. Store in a sealed container in the refrigerator for up to 2 weeks.

CAJUN GARLIC CREAM SAUCE

Originally this recipe was supposed to just be a general use sauce, but while I was shooting the cookbook with my photography dream team, someone suggested we make some pasta to go along with it. I think if this sauce had a brain, and dreams and goals, one of those dreams would be to be a pasta sauce. As a remnant of the original idea, I'm going to keep this in the sauces chapter, but if I were you, I'd make this sauce's dreams come true and pair it with a nice linguini and maybe some chicken.

2 tablespoons unsalted butter

6 garlic cloves, minced

1 cup heavy whipping cream

1 cup beef stock

½ cup store-bought Alfredo sauce

Juice of 1 fresh lemon

1 cup freshly grated Parmesan

½ cup packed roughly chopped parsley

1 tablespoon Tony Checheres Creole seasoning

1 tablespoon red chili flakes

Melt the butter in a pan over medium heat. Add the garlic and cook, stirring constantly, for 30 seconds. Whisk in the cream, the beef stock, and the Alfredo sauce and bring to a simmer. Then slowly whisk in the lemon juice. Finally stir in the Parmesan, parsley, Creole seasoning, and chili flakes. Use immediately, or it can be stored in a sealed container in the refrigerator for up to 1 week.

ALABAMA WHITE SAUCE

I love that anything can be BBQ sauce. The three main American condiments—mustard, mayonnaise, and ketchup—all have their own BBQ sauce, and they are all incredible. It's adorable. *Sidenote:* This might be my favorite of the three. It's the most versatile and can really be used on anything.

1	cup Hellmann's or Best Foods mayonnaise
¼	cup apple cider vinegar
	Juice of ½ fresh lemon
1	tablespoon Dijon mustard
1	teaspoon sugar
1	teaspoon prepared horseradish
1	teaspoon kosher salt
½	teaspoon freshly ground black pepper
¼	teaspoon cayenne

In a medium bowl, stir together the mayonnaise, vinegar, lemon, mustard, sugar, horseradish, salt, pepper, and cayenne. Store in a sealed container in the refrigerator for up to 3 weeks.

CAROLINA GOLD BBQ SAUCE

A classic mustard BBQ sauce with a spicy horseradish twist. This was my first time making this sauce; I've always loved it so much in the past, I figured I'd give it a shot, and it's incredibly easy to make.

1   cup yellow mustard

¾   cup apple cider vinegar

½   cup Hellmann's or Best Foods mayonnaise

¼   cup honey

2   tablespoons Worcestershire sauce

1   teaspoon garlic powder

1   teaspoon onion powder

1   teaspoon kosher salt

½   teaspoon smoked paprika

½   teaspoon freshly ground black pepper

¼   teaspoon cayenne

In a medium bowl, stir together the mustard, vinegar, mayonnaise, honey, Worcestershire sauce, garlic powder, onion powder, salt, paprika, pepper, and cayenne. Store in a sealed container in the refrigerator for up to 1 month.

BALSAMIC DRESSING

Everyone should have this in their repertoire. Even if you're like me and think salads are just a waste of time, at some point you'll probably have to make one. When that time comes, you're going to have the tools to make that salad sing, and everyone's gonna be like, how does Jeff from accounting who only eats steak and ice cream know how to make the best balsamic vinaigrette I've ever had? And that's when you turn to them in slow motion and say, Hank taught me, and wink. And they'll be like, okay, we don't know who Hank is, but thanks for the salad, Jeff.

¼ cup balsamic vinegar

2 garlic cloves, grated

1 teaspoon Dijon mustard
   Squeeze of fresh lemon juice

1 teaspoon kosher salt

1 teaspoon freshly ground black pepper

½ cup extra-virgin olive oil

In a medium bowl, whisk together the vinegar, garlic, mustard, lemon juice, salt, and pepper. Once they're combined, slowly drizzle the olive oil in while whisking continuously. Store in a sealed container in the refrigerator for up to 2 months.

MAKES: 2 CUPS   PREP TIME: 10 MIN   COOK TIME: N/A   TOTAL TIME: 10 MIN

CHIMICHURRI

This is my all-time favorite sauce. Don't follow the measurements—just make it however you want and it will probably still turn out amazing. Err on the side of more vinegar and you should be in good shape. Good with meat, sandwiches, salads, protein bowls, and it makes a phenomenal marinade for grilling. If you're using it for this purpose, let it marinate for at least 3 hours.

1	bunch fresh cilantro leaves, roughly chopped
1	bunch fresh parsley leaves, roughly chopped
1	large shallot, finely minced
3	garlic cloves, finely minced
1½	Fresno peppers, finely minced
1	cup white wine vinegar
⅔	cup extra-virgin olive oil
½	cup orange juice
	Juice of 1 fresh lemon
1	tablespoon dried oregano
	Pinch kosher salt
	Pinch freshly ground black pepper

In a large bowl, combine the cilantro, parsley, shallot, garlic, and peppers. Stir in the vinegar, oil, orange juice, lemon juice, oregano, salt, and pepper. Store in a sealed container in the refrigerator for up to 2 weeks.

PESTO

You might notice that this pesto is spicy. That's because there's enough garlic in there to keep you from getting laid for a year. It's the only way I ever make pesto, and if it tastes bitter, just keep adding salt until it doesn't.

- 2 **cups packed fresh basil leaves**
- 1 **cup grated Parmesan**
- ¾ **cup extra-virgin olive oil**
- ½ **cup pine nuts**
- 6 **garlic cloves**
- 2 **teaspoons kosher salt**

In a food processor or blender, combine the basil, Parmesan, olive oil, pine nuts, garlic, and salt. Blend until smooth. Store in a sealed container in the refrigerator for up to 2 weeks.

SAMBAL

If you only read one of my headnotes, let it be this one. This sauce changed my life and that's not hyperbole. Before I tell you a drawn-out story of how I became acquainted with sambal, I'll give you the high-level details. It's an Indonesian ground chili sauce that's traditionally made with garlic, shallots, lime, shrimp paste, vinegar, and hot peppers. It's been around for hundreds of years now and it's my favorite hot sauce of all time.

It's kind of a fun story, so here ya go . . . when I was twenty-four, I was working a sales job that I hated, and in a blaze of glory, I quit and booked a one-way ticket to Bangkok. The plan was to go on a food pilgrimage through as many countries as possible with the six grand I had saved up from my shitty sales job. I started my trip in Sipura, a remote island off the west coast of Indonesia. I knew this would be the cheapest way to begin my adventure, because I had a buddy who had moved there that I could stay with. He lived in a house that he built in the jungle with two locals named Anton and Terti. When I say jungle, I mean spiders-the-size-of-your-head, snakes-in-your-house, machete-hacking-your-way-through-trees jungle. Anton and Terti caught or gathered most of what we ate, and we were miles away from the nearest road or town, but they had grown up in indigenous tribes on a neighboring island, so we were in good hands. During the day we'd basically just surf and explore, and at night we'd spear frogs and set traps for mud crabs. One night one of their dogs killed a Komodo dragon (the biggest species of lizard in the world) and brought it up to the house. Just plopped a five-foot venomous lizard on the doorstep. It was a little treacherous, but it was the best kind of island living I could ever imagine.

When I first arrived, I naively expected the food to have a pretty moderate flavor profile. Anton and Terti had a little flock of chickens and a small catfish pond. They also fished and foraged daily, so I knew the food would be fresh, but within the first day I realized how much I had underestimated what these boys could do with the limited ingredients they had. In particular there was this one specific sauce. This one sauce changed my life forever. Every meal would consist of a protein on a bed of rice and veggies. This platter would come accompanied by one bowl each of red and green, freshly made, spicy-ass, homemade sambal. At the time I didn't know what it was, but after I took my first bite, it basically consumed my life. I'd watch them make it every day and harass Anton to let me film him cook. Every day they'd make more than the day before because I always licked those sambal bowls clean. I'd eat it like soup if I ran out of food to use it on.

It was one of the most impressive things that I've ever witnessed. Their families have lived in the Mentawai Islands for thousands of years and have a deep understanding of the island ingredients. The islands themselves are a thick, tall jungle that falls directly into the ocean, and Anton and Terti were experts on every plant and animal, particularly the ones that tasted good.

CONTINUES

Very unfortunately for us all, that was over five years ago and I have no idea how to get ahold of Anton. I'm sure someone is enjoying his special sambal recipe tonight, but for now it won't be us. In the meantime, here's the best imitation I can come up with. It's still damn good.

If you see this, thank you, Spencer, Anton, and Terti. Please send me that recipe. Love you boys.

20 Thai chili peppers, finely minced

18 garlic cloves, roughly chopped

3 tablespoons flaky salt

2 large shallots, finely minced

1 teaspoon shrimp paste (very optional)

2 tablespoons fresh lime juice

2 tablespoons white vinegar

Put your chilis, garlic, and salt in a mortar and pestle and grind into a paste. Add the shallots and shrimp paste, if desired, and continue to grind. Add the lime juice and vinegar and grind one final time until everything is fully ground and combined into a sauce. Store in a sealed container in the refrigerator for up to 2 weeks.

NOTE: Just a heads-up—the shrimp paste is labeled very optional because while it is traditional in some sambals, it is a pungently fishy ingredient. Once ground in with the other ingredients it adds a delicious fermented flavor, but by itself it might be off-putting to some.

CHARRED RED SALSA

When I say charred, I'm not fuckin' around. I worked at a restaurant in Oaxaca for a little while where they burnt the ingredients completely black for their sauces, and everything always came out perfectly. Feel free to char your onions, tomatoes, and peppers to varying degrees—and if you fall asleep while they're in the oven, the salsa might actually come out better.

6	**organic tomatoes**
½	**white onion**
1	**fresh jalapeño**
4	**teaspoons vegetable oil**
2	**teaspoons kosher salt**
½	**cup packed roughly chopped fresh cilantro with stems**
5	**garlic cloves**
1	**tablespoon chicken bouillon powder**

Preheat the broiler.

Coat your tomatoes, onion, and jalapeño in the oil, then generously season them with the salt. Arrange them on a sheet pan, place it under the broiler, and broil them until deeply charred, flipping halfway through, 10 to 15 minutes total. Your vegetables should be blackened on both sides.

Put the charred tomatoes, onion, and jalapeño in a blender, along with any remaining juices on the sheet pan. Add the fresh cilantro, garlic, chicken bouillon, and a splash of water and blend until it's your desired consistency. Store in a sealed container in the refrigerator for up to 1 week.

CHARRED TOMATILLO SALSA

The secret here is the bouillon—and not being afraid of over-charring. It's going to look burnt, but I promise it won't taste burnt. If you don't believe me, absolutely char the crap out of everything and I will bet you it still tastes good.

6	tomatillos, husks removed and washed
½	white onion
1	fresh jalapeño
2	tablespoons extra-virgin olive oil
1	teaspoon kosher salt
½	bunch fresh cilantro with stems
5	garlic cloves
1	tablespoon chicken bouillon powder

Preheat the broiler.

Toss the tomatillos, onion, and jalapeño in the olive oil and salt. Place them under the broiler and broil until deeply charred, flipping halfway through, 10 to 15 minutes total. Your vegetables should be blackened on both sides.

Place the vegetables in a food processor. Add the cilantro, garlic, chicken bouillon, and a splash of water and process until it's your desired consistency. Store in a sealed container in the refrigerator for up to 1 week.

FRESH GREEN SALSA

So fresh, so bright, so easy to make, and so perfect for steak tacos on a summer day. The uncooked tomatillos already have a tangy, citrus-like flavor, so there's really no need for lime juice, and as always, the bouillon pulls it all together into a flavorful work of art.

5	**tomatillos, husks removed and washed**
½	**white onion**
½	**cup packed roughly chopped fresh cilantro with stems**
4	**garlic cloves**
1	**fresh serrano pepper**
1	**tablespoon chicken bouillon powder**

In a food processor, combine the tomatillos, onion, cilantro, garlic, serrano, and bouillon and blend with ½ cup of water until smooth. Store in a sealed container in the refrigerator for up to 1 week.

BENNY BLANCO'S AVOCADO SALSA

Benny came over to make a birria sandwich and we needed something extra special to brighten it up. So he had the bright idea to whip up a nice tangy avocado salsa. This is still one of my favorite salsas of all time. THANKS, BENNY BOY!

2   **avocados, pitted, peeled, and scooped**
5   **garlic cloves**
     Juice of 2 fresh limes
1   **large fresh serrano pepper**
½   **tablespoon kosher salt**
1   **cup canola oil**

Put the avocados, garlic, lime juice, pepper, and salt in a food processor. Blend the mixture while slowly adding the oil, until the consistency reaches a loose mayonnaise texture.

Enjoy on tacos or with tortilla chips. Store in a sealed container in the refrigerator for up to 1 week with lime squirted on top to keep it fresh and green.

GUACAMOLE

I know I'm going to catch some heat for the simplicity of this guac, but I simply can't ignore how good it is, even in the name of tradition. If it makes this less controversial, we can just call it avocado-lemon-garlic-salt dip and spread. But it's guacamole.

2   **avocados, pitted, peeled, and scooped**

2   **garlic cloves, grated**

     Juice of ½ fresh lemon

2   **teaspoons kosher salt**

In a medium bowl, mash your avocados with the garlic, lemon juice, and salt. Store in a sealed container in the refrigerator for up to 1 week with lime squirted on top to keep it fresh and green.

FRENCH ONION DIP

Clearly, I have some weird obsession with this Caramelized Onion recipe, but I think it's justified. I'm gonna level with you guys, using the onions in a dip was an afterthought. They popped up in so many other places in this book that while writing the dips chapter I was like, wait. Hold up. Oh my god yes. It may have been an afterthought, but sometimes those things that you didn't see coming are the most special of all <3.

It's a caramelized onion dip—what's not to like?

1 pound cream cheese

2 cups sour cream

3½ cups (1 recipe) Caramelized Onions (recipe follows)

2 cups grated Gruyère cheese

⅓ cup thinly sliced fresh chives, for garnish

Crusty baguette crostinis (see Note), for serving

Preheat the broiler.

Combine the cream cheese and sour cream with the Caramelized Onions in a medium cast iron skillet over medium heat. Stir to combine, then sprinkle the grated Gruyère over the top. Broil until the Gruyère starts to brown and bubble on top, about 5 minutes. Garnish with the chives and serve with crostinis.

NOTE: Preheat the oven to 300°F and line a sheet pan with parchment paper. Slice a baguette on the bias and spread the slices out on the sheet pan. Brush the slices using a few tablespoons of olive oil, then bake until golden brown and crunchy, about 30 minutes.

CARAMELIZED ONIONS

½ cup (1 stick) unsalted butter

2 tablespoons extra-virgin olive oil

2 yellow onions, thinly sliced

2 red onions, thinly sliced

2 white onions, thinly sliced

1½ tablespoons plus 1 pinch kosher salt, divided

1 tablespoon freshly ground black pepper

½ cup Worcestershire sauce

1½ cups (½ bottle) dry red wine, dry cabernet works well

In a large saucepan over medium to medium-low heat, place the butter and the olive oil. Once the butter is melted, add the sliced onions. Season with 1½ tablespoons of the salt and the freshly ground black pepper and mix everything together. Allow the onions to slowly start to caramelize, stirring occasionally. As they start to take on some color, after about 30 minutes, add the Worcestershire sauce. Mix everything to combine and continue to caramelize. Make sure to stir the onions every 5 minutes to avoid burning. Once the onions are almost fully caramelized, about 1 hour into the overall cooking, add the wine and a generous pinch of salt. Cook until the wine is reduced all the way down and the onions are dark brown and reach a sticky, mushy texture, about 30 more minutes. Remove them from heat and set aside. Serve immediately, or the onions can be stored in a sealed container in the refrigerator for up to 2 weeks.

MAKES: 3½ CUPS

PREP TIME: 10 MIN

COOK TIME: 1 HR 30 MIN

TOTAL TIME:
1 HR 40 MIN

SOUR CREAM AND CHIVE DIP

I used to gobble this shit down at my friend's house. Not this homemade one specifically, the kind that comes in a Lay's jar, which I'm basically trying to re-create. My mom refused to buy stuff that wasn't organic, so I'd have it at my buddy Sean's house. His mom always kept the fridge and pantry fully stocked with fire snacks. I think most people had a friend like that growing up. To this day I could probably show up to Sean's and be welcomed with some gushers, Doritos, and a plate of steak tacos. Love you, Kathy.

2   cups sour cream
½   cup thinly sliced fresh chives
2   garlic cloves, minced
2½ teaspoons kosher salt
2   teaspoons freshly ground black pepper
2   teaspoons apple cider vinegar
1   teaspoon Worcestershire sauce
1   teaspoon onion powder

In a medium bowl, combine the sour cream, chives, garlic, salt, pepper, vinegar, Worcestershire sauce, and onion powder. Stir well and serve with potato chips. It can be stored in a sealed container in the refrigerator for up to 2 weeks.

WHIPPED FETA

Without this dip/spread I wouldn't be where I am today. It's one of the main components of my baby, my first viral recipe ever, the lamb burger. And I have a huge confession to make. I'm a gigantic fraud. The lamb burger was entirely my friend Jerry's idea. We always used to brainstorm shit to make, and one day he sent over a pretty comprehensive idea for a lamb burger with whipped feta, pickled onions, harissa mayo, and arugula. Before even filming the video, I knew it was going to crush, but without Jerry's text I wouldn't have come up with that idea in a billion years. One hundred million views later and he hasn't complained once. What a guy. I still feel it's necessary to finally thank him and come clean about this masterpiece of a recipe. THANKS, JERRY, LOVE YA, BUD.

2   cups crumbled feta

1   cup cream cheese, cut into cubes

2   garlic bulbs, roasted (see Note) plus 4 garlic cloves, roughly minced

½   cup extra-virgin olive oil

½   cup fresh mint leaves

½   cup roughly sliced fresh chives

    Juice of 1 fresh lemon

In a food processor, combine the feta, cream cheese, garlic, olive oil, mint, chives, and lemon juice, and blend until smooth. Store in a sealed container in the refrigerator for up to 2 weeks.

NOTE: To roast the garlic bulbs, wrap them in foil and roast in a 400°F oven for 1 hour. Squeeze the softened garlic cloves out of their skins when done.

SOUR CREAM AND CHIVE
DIP, PAGE 178

WHIPPED FETA,
PAGE 179

CHARRED RED SALSA, PAGE 171

SPINACH ARTICHOKE DIP

I think most of us can agree this is the king of all dips. One of my favorites growing up, yet again because of a friend's mom. Peggy, you get all the credit for this one. Thinking of the days we'd be playing full-contact mini-hoop basketball in that room by the front door, then go sit down and eat a full container of spinach artichoke dip. Peak nostalgia.

1 tablespoon extra-virgin olive oil

1 shallot, minced

1 tablespoon minced garlic

1 teaspoon crushed red chili flakes (optional)

1½ teaspoons kosher salt

½ teaspoon freshly ground black pepper

6 cups fresh, packed spinach leaves

1 (14-ounce) can artichoke hearts, drained and chopped

1 pound cream cheese

½ cup sour cream

½ cup Hellmann's or Best Foods mayonnaise

½ cup shredded mozzarella cheese

1 cup grated Parmesan
   Crostini, for serving

In a skillet over medium heat, heat the olive oil and add the shallot, garlic, and red chili flakes, if desired. Cook, stirring constantly, until the shallot begins to become translucent, 2 to 3 minutes. Season with the salt and pepper, then add the spinach and cook, stirring frequently, until it's cooked all the way down, 3 to 4 minutes.

Transfer the spinach mixture to a blender, then add the chopped artichoke hearts, cream cheese, sour cream, and mayonnaise. Pulse to combine, then transfer it to a roasting dish. Sprinkle the mozzarella and Parmesan on top, then place the dip under the broiler until the mozzarella starts to caramelize and form golden-brown bubbles on top, about 7 minutes. Serve with crostini. It can be stored in a sealed container in the refrigerator for up to 2 weeks.

WHIPPED PÂTÉ DIP

This was originally conceived just to add a little pizazz to the pâté for our Banh Mi Dip sandwich (page 229), but immediately after making it I almost felt bad putting it on a sandwich. It EASILY can stand on its own as a dip or spread. Most pâtés have a harder, colder consistency and require a butter knife for spreading, whereas this goes through the food processor with the mayonnaise, giving it almost a hummus-like consistency. If you have friends who are a little apprehensive about the idea of eating pâté straight, this is like pâté with training wheels for your average consumer. It also just tastes better with the garlic, chili, and mayo. By the way, I'm not putting down pâté. I looooove pâté by itself; this is just a completely different thing.

2   garlic cloves
1   Fresno chili pepper
1½ teaspoons kosher salt
    Pork and duck liver pâté, totaling 10 ounces
3   heaping tablespoons Hellmann's or Best Foods mayonnaise
½   cup thinly sliced fresh chives, for garnish

Put the garlic, pepper, and salt into a food processor. Blitz until everything is minced and then scrape down the sides. Add the pâté and mayonnaise and blend until smooth.

Serve in a bowl garnished with sliced chives. It can be stored in a sealed container in the refrigerator for up to 1 week.

FERMENTED AND PICKLED

I'M NOT AN EXPERT ON EITHER OF THESE, but I'm definitely obsessed with both. I started pickling shit in college when I had seven roommates, and for some reason nobody seemed to appreciate it as much as I did. I didn't really know what I was doing; I'd basically just put sliced onions in a bowl with red wine vinegar and put them in the fridge. Now that I'm further along, I still do that all the time. There are a million ways to attack this, but here is some general knowledge for both.

Quick pickling is basically packing vegetables in a jar with vinegar and salt brine and letting them sit for like four plus hours. It can definitely help preserve stuff, but it doesn't give you the long-term shelf-stable final product that fermentation does. This is mostly about the flavor. You can pickle basically anything, especially vegetables. Just boil vinegar and water with a big pinch of salt and whatever other spices you want, pack a jar with your prepped ingredients, and pour the brine over them. The type of vinegar you use is totally up to you and is the most fun thing to play around with for these recipes. Some common spices to use are peppercorns, mustard seed, red chili flakes, fennel seed, bay leaf, coriander seed, and a giant variety of other stuff. You can add sugar, but I don't use it often—unless you like bread-and-butter pickles or are making pickled daikon and carrots, in which case go to town.

Fermentation might be the most interesting method of cooking, historically. It changed the game in so many ways and has meant life or death in a lot of ways for thousands of years. Fermentation wasn't as much a fun hobby as it was a means of survival in those circumstances. People would make a gigantic batch of kimchi to last their families through the winter months, and if they messed something up and the kimchi spoiled, big-ass whoopsie. Pirates' life spans increased significantly when they figured out how to preserve lemons and limes to prevent scurvy. Like, by a gigantic margin. Fermenting has such a long, wild history and is still one of the only ways to achieve that fermented, tangy flavor. A general rule, if you want to ferment something, is pack it in a jar with a 3–5 percent kosher salt brine, top it with a fermentation weight (which is something that holds the vegetables under the brine to keep them from being exposed to the outside air), and cover the top with cheesecloth sealed by a rubber band. Put it in a dark, coldish place and let it ferment for anywhere from a week to a couple months. You'll need to skim the mold off the top every other day or so. BTW, 3–5 percent salt brine means whatever the water weighs, add 3–5 percent of that weight in kosher salt and mix until dissolved. This method applies to pickles, sauerkraut, peppers for hot sauce, and most other fermented delicacies.

PICKLED ONIONS

This is where it all started, where my love for pickling began. Onions were the only thing I knew how to pickle until I was like twenty, and I didn't even really know how to pickle them. I'd just put sliced onions in a bowl with vinegar (and honestly it works just as well). I have a giant jar of these in my fridge at all times and you should too.

2	medium red onions
3½	cups white wine vinegar
1½	cups water
2	tablespoons Pickling Spice Blend (see Note, page 193)
2	tablespoons non-iodized sea salt
½	tablespoon granulated sugar
1	tablespoon dried oregano

Using a mandoline, slice your onions on setting #2, or ⅛-inch thick. Stuff them into a heatproof container, ideally a 32-ounce Mason jar.

In a medium saucepan over high heat, bring the vinegar, water, Pickling Spice Blend, salt, and sugar to a boil. Pour the mixture over your onions, stir in the oregano, and let them sit in the fridge for 12 hours, and up to 2 months.

GIARDINIERA

This is my top favorite pickling recipe, and I'm not necessarily talking about giardiniera. There are a ton of variations of this style of pickled vegetable. In the Middle East it's called torshi, and depending on the region it can include a huge range of different vegetables and spices. I have a friend from Iran who told me her family doesn't consider a meal complete without a communal bowl of torshi. Giardiniera, however, holds a very special place in my heart. The very first sandwich I learned how to make (that wasn't, like, a PB&J) was a muffuletta, and giardiniera is the most important ingredient in that sandwich. My dad taught me how to make it when I was a kid, and I've been obsessed ever since. Like I mentioned, this recipe is so endlessly customizable—you could sub in or sub out almost any of the vegetables for things you like more, or even do a version that just includes two things. One of my favorite jarred hot peppers is made using this method, but it's just peppers, with a bit of garlic and celery for flavor.

2	cups cauliflower florets
2	large carrots, sliced into ¼-inch pieces
2	celery stalks, sliced into ¼-inch pieces
5	fresh serrano peppers, sliced into ¼-inch pieces
8	smashed garlic cloves
4	cups white wine vinegar
2	cups water
2	tablespoons non-iodized sea salt
2	teaspoons mustard seeds
2	teaspoons coriander seeds
2	teaspoons fennel seeds
2	bay leaves
2	cups extra-virgin olive oil

In a large pot over medium-high heat, combine the cauliflower, carrots, celery, serranos, and garlic with the vinegar, water, salt, mustard seeds, coriander seeds, fennel seeds, and bay leaves. Bring to a boil and cook for 5 minutes, then kill the heat. Transfer your veggies to a large Mason jar and pour the brine over them.

Let the veggies pickle for 24 hours, then strain out the brine and replace it in the jar with your olive oil. Seal and store in the fridge for up to 2 months.

QUICK DILL PICKLES

It's a pickle, you get it. I will say, however, once you start making your own pickles, you will probably never stop. It's this fun little science project that takes minimal effort but yields such impressive results. These aren't fermented and that's on purpose. Fermenting takes longer and you need homemade pickles, like, yesterday. Happy pickling.

12 **medium cucumbers, quartered lengthwise and cut to fit jar**

3 **sprigs fresh dill**

6 **garlic cloves, peeled and smashed**

1 **fresh habanero pepper, halved**

3½ **cups distilled white vinegar**

1½ **cups water**

2 **large tablespoons non-iodized sea salt**

2 **tablespoons Pickling Spice Blend (see Note)**

½ **tablespoon granulated sugar**

Add your cucumber spears to a 32-ounce Mason jar, along with the dill, garlic, and habanero.

Combine the vinegar, water, salt, Pickling Spice Blend, and sugar in a medium pot over high heat and bring to a boil. Lower heat to a simmer for 2 minutes. Let brine cool, then pour over the cucumber spears and seal your container. If there's leftover brine, use a spoon to scoop the remaining pickling spices into the jar.

Let sit in the fridge for at least 24 hours and up to 2 months.

NOTE: For the Pickling Spice Blend, use what you have or prefer of these ingredients: black peppercorns, coriander seed, mustard seed, caraway seed, dill seed, fennel, red pepper flakes, dill seed, and a bay leaf.

PICKLED GARLIC

Two things here—please don't ever buy preserved garlic, ever, in any situation. That means the pre-minced shit in jars or the vacuum-sealed cloves. There are bags of garlic that are freshly peeled, and those work totally fine, but make sure they're not preserved. I'm also gonna sneak another recipe into this intro without telling my editor. I'm assuming if you've made it this far, you're probably a big fan of garlic, so here's garlic sauce: blend 20 to 30 garlic cloves with olive oil, lemon juice, and salt. This can be used as a sauce or just as an ingredient when you need minced garlic. Use a lot of salt, and as much oil as it takes for the sauce to reach a pesto-like consistency.

Cloves from 4 garlic bulbs, peeled (or enough to fill your jar)

2   **cups white vinegar**

½   **cup water**

1   **tablespoon non-iodized sea salt**

2   **teaspoons red chili flakes**

Pack the peeled garlic cloves into a heatproof container.

In a medium saucepan over high heat, combine the vinegar, water, salt, and red chili flakes and bring to a boil. Pour the liquid over your garlic and seal the jar.

Prepare a large pot of boiling water. Submerge the jar in the boiling water for 10 minutes.

Remove the jar and store it in a cool, dark area for 2 to 3 weeks before opening.

Once it's been opened, store in the fridge for up to 2 months.

PICKLED GINGER, OR GARI

You've probably had this a million times if you eat sushi. It's great for gut health and great for flavoring food. If you're one of the people that eats this before the sushi actually gets to the table, now you can have it at home and snack on it all day.

½ **pound fresh, young ginger**
1 **cup rice vinegar**
½ **cup sugar**
1 **teaspoon non-iodized sea salt**

Using a spoon, scrape the skin off of the ginger. Once it's peeled, thinly slice the ginger using a mandoline. The slices should be paper thin.

Bring a medium saucepan of water to a boil over high heat. Add the ginger and boil for about 30 seconds, then strain it from water. Place the ginger in a 32-ounce Mason jar.

In a medium saucepan over medium heat, combine the rice vinegar, sugar, and salt and bring to a light simmer, stirring to dissolve the sugar. Set it aside to cool, then pour it over your ginger. Make sure the ginger is fully submerged. Close your jar and refrigerate it for at least 24 hours before using, and store in the refrigerator for up to 2 months.

PICKLED JICAMA

This one is special. Jicama has such a mild flavor that when you pickle it you basically just get a crunchy vinegar sponge. What would you do with a crunchy vinegar sponge? Eat it straight? Add it to a salad? Use it to get a stain out? The options are endless, and I always have something like this in my fridge. Use it to brighten up ANYTHING that feels like it's lacking some tang or acidity. Make this and I bet you'll end up just snacking on it.

3	medium jicamas, peeled and julienned
2	garlic cloves, smashed
1	teaspoon whole black peppercorns
1	teaspoon red chili flakes
3	cups apple cider vinegar
1	cup water
3	tablespoons sugar
2	tablespoons non-iodized sea salt

Put the jicama in a 32-ounce Mason jar, along with the garlic, peppercorns, and red chili flakes.

In a medium saucepan over high heat, combine the vinegar, water, sugar, and salt and bring to a quick boil. Set the mixture aside to cool, then pour it over the jicama and seal the jar.

Let it sit in fridge for at least 12 hours, and up to 2 months.

QUICK PICKLED JALAPEÑOS

These don't get the respect I think they deserve. Usually, they're served as whole slices for a topping on nachos or in a burrito, etc. My favorite way to use them is diced up in a sauce or relish, or add the brine to a beer for some tangy heat. There are a million ways to use pickled jalapeños that get ignored frequently. Get creative!!

8   fresh jalapeños, thinly sliced
3   cups white vinegar
1   cup water
1   tablespoon non-iodized sea salt
1   tablespoon sugar
1   bay leaf

Place your jalapeños in a heatproof container. In a medium saucepan over high heat, combine the vinegar, water, salt, sugar, and bay leaf. Bring the mixture to a boil, then pour over your jalapeños. After a couple hours, they're ready to use. They can be stored in a sealed container for up to 2 months.

PICKLED AND FRIED PEPPERS

Pickled peppers are part of the reason I fell in love with pickling. They're the perfect accompaniment to sandwiches, salads, bowls, etc., but when you fry them, they take on an entirely new life. I'd recommend doubling the Pickled Pepper recipe and storing half in a Mason jar for other stuff.

4   cups vegetable oil
2   cups all-purpose flour
1½   tablespoons garlic powder
1½   tablespoons onion powder
1½   tablespoons paprika
1½   tablespoons kosher salt
1½   tablespoons freshly ground pepper
1½   tablespoons dried parsley
1½   tablespoons cayenne
1   recipe Pickled Peppers (page 201)
1   cup packed fresh basil leaves
1   recipe Spicy Ranch (page 152)

Heat your oil in a large pot or deep skillet over medium heat to 350°F.

In a bowl, combine the flour, garlic powder, onion powder, paprika, salt, pepper, dried parsley, and cayenne. Mix thoroughly. Pull a handful of your peppers out of the brine and shake some of the excess brine off. Toss them in the seasoned flour and repeat until all your peppers are fully battered. Dip your lemon slices in the brine, shake them off, and batter those as well.

Carefully add the peppers and the lemon slices to the oil in batches and fry them until they are perfectly golden brown, 3 to 5 minutes. Let them drain on a paper towel or wire rack. Season them immediately after pulling them from the oil. Once you're finished with the peppers and lemons, quickly fry your basil leaves. These fry pretty violently, so be prepared for a loud noise when you put them in; once they've calmed down, immediately pull them out.

Fill a small bowl with the ranch and arrange your fried peppers and lemons around the bowl on a platter. Garnish the peppers with the fried basil.

PICKLED PEPPERS

1   pound sweet mini peppers (one of those bags)
3   fresh jalapeños
1   fresh lemon
1   tablespoon dried oregano
4   garlic cloves, crushed
3   cups apple cider vinegar
1   cup water
2½ tablespoons non-iodized sea salt

Thinly slice your sweet peppers, jalapeños, and lemon into rounds (no need to core the peppers beforehand). If you're using a mandoline, use the #3 setting. Stuff the slices into a heatproof container, ideally a 32-ounce Mason jar. Add your dried oregano and garlic.

In a medium saucepan over medium heat, bring the vinegar, water, and salt to a low boil, stirring to dissolve the salt, about 3 minutes. Pour the mixture over your peppers until everything is fully submerged. Carefully close the lid and shake your container to mix. Let it sit in the fridge for at least 4 hours, and up to 1 month.

MAKES: 1 QUART
**PREP TIME: 10 MIN PLUS
4 HRS PICKLING TIME**
COOK TIME: 3 MIN
**TOTAL TIME:
4 HRS 13 MIN**

FERMENTED HABANERO AND CARROT HOT SAUCE

Fermented hot sauce is the best hot sauce. This sauce will likely kick the ass of any other hot sauce you've had before—that is, other than Yellowbird (not sponsored, those guys just make the world's best hot sauce). The fermentation of hot sauce takes a bit of patience, but it's quite a fun project and a great introduction to the world of fermentation. Heads up, this version is very spicy, but the habaneros can be subbed for/mixed with a milder chili like Fresno or jalapeño.

½   pound fresh habanero peppers
¼   pound peeled carrots
6   garlic cloves
2   tablespoons kosher salt
½   cup distilled water
½   cup apple cider vinegar
     Sugar or honey, as needed

Rinse the peppers, removing any stems, and chop them roughly. Make sure to wash your hands after handling the *very hot* peppers. Chop your carrots into ½-inch slices and smash your garlic cloves.

Place the peppers, carrots, and garlic in a clean glass jar. Add the salt and mix everything together.

Pour the distilled water into the jar until the peppers are completely covered. Add a fermentation weight to keep the peppers submerged.

Cover the jar with a clean cloth or cheesecloth, secured with a rubber band or string.

Place the jar in a cool, dark place for a week or so. Check on the hot sauce every few days, making sure the peppers are fully submerged in the brine. Skim off any mold that may form on the surface.

After the desired fermentation time, remove the weight and discard any mold or scum on the surface. Transfer the mixture to a blender or food processor, and puree until smooth.

Add the apple cider vinegar to the hot sauce and mix.

Taste and adjust the seasoning as needed. It'll probably need some salt, and feel free to add some sugar or honey as well.

Pour the hot sauce into squirt bottles and light your ass on fire. Store in the refrigerator for up to 6 months.

SANDWICHES AND BURGERS

WE'VE FINALLY MADE IT—THE SANDWICH CHAPTER. SANDWICHES ARE the reason I got this book, and they're probably the reason you guys know who I am. I owe my entire career to meat between baguette halves. It was tough to narrow down my favorites, but I hope you guys like the selection ahead of you. If something's missing, DM me and I'll send you the raw, uncut recipe.

I am in love with you, sandwiches. You're a beacon of hope in this fucked-up world—crunchy, juicy, savory, saucy, meaty sandwiches. I'm writing this on a train to Florence, and all I can think about is the first sandwich I'm going to eat when we arrive.

Without further ado, the sandwich chapter!

SPICY VODKA PARM

Here's where I first tested the waters with compound butter on sandwiches, and to this day, I think it's one of the best food hacks ever created. A common sandwich like this comes across as pretty unassuming, but the garlicky, fatty, spicy baguette holding it all together adds more flavor than any of the other ingredients and makes for the best chicken parm sandwich you've ever had. This same compound butter applied to pretty much any Italian sandwich will hit every single time. There will be leftover sauce with this recipe—you can reserve that for a spicy rigatoni or homemade pizza.

3   tablespoons extra-virgin olive oil, plus more for drizzling

½   white onion, diced

15 Calabrian chilis, minced

6   garlic cloves, divided

1   sprig fresh basil plus 1 cup packed fresh basil leaves, divided

1   teaspoon kosher salt, plus more for seasoning

1   teaspoon freshly ground black pepper, plus more for seasoning

2   cups vodka (optional)

1   (28-ounce) can pureed tomatoes

2½ cups heavy whipping cream

½   cup (1 stick) unsalted butter, softened

1   handful fresh parsley, roughly chopped

1   sourdough or Italian baguette

2   boneless, skinless chicken breasts

3   to 4 cups vegetable oil, for frying

1   cup all-purpose flour

2   large eggs whisked with 1 tablespoon water

1½ cups panko

1   tablespoon Cajun seasoning

1   (8-ounce) ball buffalo mozzarella, sliced

3   tablespoons freshly grated Parmesan

Heat the olive oil in a large skillet over medium heat. Add the onion, 10 of the minced Calabrian chilis (i.e., ⅔ of the minced amount), 3 cloves of thinly sliced garlic, and the sprig of basil. Season with 1 teaspoon each of salt and pepper. Cook, stirring, until fragrant, 3 to 4 minutes.

(This next step is optional and doesn't really change the flavor or final outcome of the dish, but it's fun and makes you look cool.) Kill the heat and add your vodka to the skillet. Set it on fire with a long lighter or by shaking the pan back and forth if over a gas burner.

Let the vodka completely burn off, bring the pan back up to medium heat, then stir in the tomato puree. Bring the sauce to a simmer and reduce, stirring occasionally, for 10 minutes. Add the cream, mix again, and reduce until slightly thickened, for another 3 to 5 minutes. Remove from the heat and set aside.

Preheat the oven to 400°F.

In a medium bowl, mix the butter with the chopped parsley, the remaining 3 garlic cloves, minced, the remaining Calabrian chilis, and big pinches of salt and freshly ground pepper. Spread thick layers of your compound butter on both halves of your baguette and place in the oven butter side up until melted and toasted, 5 to 7 minutes.

CONTINUES

Put your chicken breasts between two layers of parchment paper and tenderize until the entire breast is ¼ to ½ inch thick.

Fill a deep skillet up with ½ inch of vegetable oil and heat for 10 minutes over medium heat.

Put your flour, egg wash, and the panko mixed with the Cajun seasoning into separate shallow bowls for dredging. Batter the chicken first in flour, then egg wash, then seasoned panko.

Fry the chicken until browned and cooked through, a total of 8 to 10 minutes, flipping halfway through and basting exposed areas with oil. Place on a wire rack over a sheet pan. Spread a thick layer of your vodka sauce and slices of mozzarella on top of the chicken. Place under the broiler until the mozzarella starts to bubble and turn golden brown.

To build your sandwich, on one side of your compound butter toast, layer the vodka sauce, then your broiled chicken and cheese. Add the fresh basil leaves, along with a drizzle of olive oil, salt, pepper, and finally some grated Parmesan. Top with the other compound butter toast and enjoy.

SPICY VODKA PARM, CONTINUED

ORANGE CHICKEN SANDWICH

Big shout-out to Panda Express for inventing orange chicken. People might not believe that, but its google-able. The orange chicken sauce in this sandwich is tangy and thick, but the brine from the cucumber salad cuts right through it. If you're a fan of Panda Express, I think you'll like this a lot. And if you're not, I still think you'll like this a lot. This might've been the unanimously favorite sandwich out of everyone who helped with this book, and they are pros whose job it is to eat other people's food, so it's very credible testimony.

FOR THE CUCUMBER SALAD

- **2   tablespoons minced garlic**
- **1   tablespoon soy sauce**
- **1   tablespoon furikake**
- **1   teaspoon kosher salt**
- **1   teaspoon sesame oil**
- **1   cup very thinly sliced cucumber**
- **2   Fresno chilis, sliced very thinly**
- **½   cup thinly sliced red onions**

FOR THE ORANGE CHICKEN SAUCE

- **½   cup orange juice**
- **Grated zest of 1 orange**
- **2   tablespoons soy sauce**
- **2   tablespoons honey**
- **1   tablespoon rice vinegar**
- **1   tablespoon cornstarch whisked in 1 tablespoon water**
- **1   Fresno chili, minced**
- **1   teaspoon grated ginger**
- **1   garlic clove, minced**

FOR THE CHICKEN

- **1   cup all-purpose flour**
- **½   cup potato or corn starch**
- **1   tablespoon paprika**
- **1   tablespoon cayenne**
- **1   tablespoon kosher salt**
- **1   tablespoon freshly ground black pepper**
- **1   tablespoon onion powder**
- **1   tablespoon garlic powder**
- **2   chicken thighs**
- **2   cups buttermilk**
- **2   cups vegetable oil**
- **2   tablespoons unsalted butter**
- **2   sandwich buns**

CONTINUES

MAKE THE CUCUMBER SALAD: In a medium bowl, whisk together the garlic, soy sauce, furikake, salt, and sesame oil. Add the cucumber, Fresno chilis, and red onion and toss to coat. Set aside in the refrigerator.

MAKE THE ORANGE CHICKEN SAUCE: In a small saucepan over high heat, combine the orange juice, orange zest, soy sauce, honey, rice vinegar, cornstarch slurry, Fresno chili, ginger, and garlic and bring to a full boil. Reduce heat to medium-low and simmer, stirring occasionally, until the mixture reaches a syrupy consistency, about 3 minutes. Add more cornstarch to make it thicker, if needed. Set aside.

MAKE THE CHICKEN: In a medium bowl, season the flour and starch with the paprika, cayenne, salt, pepper, onion powder, and garlic powder.

Brine the chicken in the buttermilk for 3 hours if possible (but the full 3 hours is not required).

In a medium pot or deep skillet over medium heat, heat the oil to 350°F.

Remove the chicken from the buttermilk and then coat it in the seasoned flour, making sure to press the flour firmly into the thighs and to not miss any spots.

Fry the chicken until golden brown, 8 to 12 minutes, flipping halfway through. Remove and let rest on a rack.

Butter and toast your buns.

Using a brush or spoon, slather the chicken in the orange chicken sauce.

BUILD YOUR SANDWICH: Add a pile of your cucumber salad to the bottom buns, then add your sauced orange chicken. Add a couple extra spoonfuls of orange chicken sauce on top and eat.

PESTO CHICKEN SANDWICH

One of my all-time favorite sandwiches . . . I'm now realizing I'm probably going to accidentally write that for every single sandwich in this book. That isn't necessarily a bad thing; the sandwiches in this book are the culmination of hundreds of sandwich trials, and we are left with the best sixteen sandwiches I've ever made. Even so, this sandwich is still probably top five.

1	cup arugula
1	cup thinly sliced red onion
2	tablespoons extra-virgin olive oil
	Juice of ½ fresh lemon
3	tablespoons red wine vinegar
1	teaspoon kosher salt
1	teaspoon freshly ground black pepper
2	boneless, skinless chicken breasts
1	tablespoon vegetable oil
1	tablespoon Tony Checheres Creole seasoning
1	rustic baguette, sliced open and toasted
	Calabrian Chili Garlic Aioli (page 150)
	Pesto (page 167)
3	slices provolone cheese
1	organic heirloom tomato, sliced medium thick
	Pickled Peppers (page 201)

Preheat the oven to 375°F.

Mix the arugula, onion, olive oil, lemon juice, vinegar, salt, and pepper in a medium bowl. Set aside.

Generously brush your chicken breasts with vegetable oil and coat them with your Creole seasoning. Heat a medium pan over medium heat, then sear the chicken, 5 minutes each side, and finish cooking in the oven, 7 to 10 minutes. Slice the chicken into ½-inch strips.

Preheat the broiler.

On the bottom half of your toasted, rustic baguette, heavily slather on the Calabrian garlic mayo followed by a large portion of your onion arugula salad, then your sliced chicken. Spoon large globs of pesto on top of the chicken, then top that with the provolone. Broil until the cheese is fully melted, then layer on the sliced heirloom tomato and Pickled Peppers. Close the sandwich with the top of the baguette and serve.

ROAST CHICKEN SOUP SANDWICH

This is just taking the roast chicken recipe and putting it between bread. I know that sounds lazy, but giving that broth, those pan juices, a place to live is incredibly important. The bread soaks in all that lost flavor from the bottom of the roasting dish, flavor that is hard to capture when you're just eating the chicken by itself. Here you've got all the flavors from this roast chicken between two pieces of bread, and adding the crispy chicken skin and roasted veggies is something entirely new and worthy of its own headnote. If you make the roast chicken, try one of these out too and I bet you'll agree.

1   **rustic baguette**
1   **whole roast chicken from the Roast Chicken
     and Garlic Bread recipe (page 132)**
     **Veggies cooked under the chicken, minus the
     potatoes, sliced**
     Juices from the bottom of the roasting dish
     Kosher salt, for seasoning

Toast your baguette.

Pull the meat and crispy skin off your chicken and load it onto your baguette. Fill the rest of the baguette with the roasted carrots, onion, celery, and garlic.

Ladle the juices all over everything, allowing the toasted baguette to soak some of it up. Season with a sprinkle of kosher salt. Serve!

MUFFULETTA

This has been one of my favorite sandwiches since I was a kid. It was the first hot sandwich I ever learned how to make. My dad taught me when I was like ten, after he had made them for dinner one night. I was obsessed, and we ended up having weekly muffuletta nights for years. Definitely one of those nostalgic comfort foods for your boy. This might be the only sandwich that can really get away with not having any kind of sauce or lubricant on it. I guess the olive salad has moisture, but this thing could hang out in your fridge and be totally fine to grill up and eat like a week later.

2	red bell peppers
1½	tablespoons extra-virgin olive oil, divided
1	teaspoon kosher salt
1	teaspoon freshly ground black pepper
1	cup giardiniera (store-bought or see page 192)
1	cup pimiento olives
1	cup Kalamata olives
1	cup pepperoncini
1	rustic baguette
½	pound sliced salami (your favorite kind)
½	pound sliced provolone cheese
½	pound sliced ham (your favorite kind)
½	pound sliced mortadella

Preheat the oven to 400°F.

To roast the red peppers, remove the core and rub with ½ tablespoon of the olive oil, the salt, and the pepper. Place on a sheet pan and roast for 15 to 20 minutes.

Put the peppers, giardiniera, pimento olives, Kalamata olives, and pepperoncini in a blender and blend until minced. You now have your muffuletta mix.

Add a hefty layer of your olive salad mix to the bottom of your baguette, followed by a layer of salami, cheese, ham, cheese, mortadella, cheese, and finally more olive salad mix. You can make this sandwich as big as you want, by the way.

Next, heat the remaining 1 tablespoon of olive oil in a skillet over medium heat and cook the sandwich like you would a panini. Add the sandwich, then place something heavy on top and press down firmly. After 3 to 4 minutes repeat on the other side. Chances are the cheese isn't going to fully melt, but that's totally fine. Enjoy your muffuletta.

NOTE: To make the olive salad, you can use the giardiniera from the book or store-bought. Either way, you'll be blending it all together with roasted red peppers and other briny ingredients.

HOT COD SANDWICH

Hot Cod Sandwich, baby. Another quick shout-out to my buddy boy Jerry for suggesting this one. It's basically a Nashville Hot chicken sandwich, but with fish instead of chicken. This batter technique is courtesy of Stephen Cusato from *Not Another Cooking Show* on YouTube, who credits Heston Blumenthal, a British chef/food genius, with the original recipe. The vodka evaporates and creates small, cavernous areas in the batter, which make for the most uniquely crunchy fried thing I've ever eaten, and I recommend you look up Stephen's video about it on YouTube. If you'd rather keep it simple and avoid all that scientific shit, scrap the vodka, dip it in wet batter, and then coat it in seasoned flour, which will solidify the outside a lot more than just having wet batter. That's actually what we did for the fish in this photograph, 'cause I screwed up the batter that day lol. Whichever way you hack it, the final product will be incredible.

FOR THE WET BATTER

- 2 cups all-purpose flour
- 1 cup rice flour
- 2 tablespoons baking powder
- 1 cup vodka
- 1 (11.2-ounce) bottle pilsner beer
- 1 tablespoon honey

FOR THE SIMPLE SLAW

- 1 cup thinly sliced white cabbage
- 1 cup thinly sliced red onion
- 3 tablespoons apple cider vinegar

FOR THE NASHVILLE HOT

- 5 teaspoons cayenne
- 1 teaspoon paprika
- 1 teaspoon sugar
- 1 teaspoon kosher salt
- 1 teaspoon garlic powder
- 1 teaspoon onion powder

FOR THE FISH

- 2 cups vegetable oil
- 2 (8-ounce) cod fillets
  Kosher salt, for seasoning
  Freshly ground black pepper, for seasoning
- 2 tablespoons unsalted butter
- 2 sandwich buns
  Creole Remoulade (page 149), for garnish
  Quick Dill Pickles (page 193), sliced for garnish

CONTINUES

MAKE THE WET BATTER: In a bowl, stir together the all-purpose flour, rice flour, and baking powder. Stir in the vodka, half of the beer, and the honey. Add more beer until you have the right consistency; it should come out like a loose pancake batter. Adjust by adding more or less beer. I generally find it comes to just a bit shy of a full bottle. Set the batter aside.

MAKE THE SLAW: In a separate bowl, toss together the cabbage, red onion, and apple cider vinegar to make your slaw. Set aside.

MAKE THE NASHVILLE HOT: In a medium bowl, stir together the cayenne, paprika, sugar, salt, garlic powder, and onion powder. Set aside.

MAKE THE FISH: In a pot or deep skillet heat your oil up to 350°F.

Season your cod fillets with salt and pepper.

Carefully dip your cod in the wet batter, and without losing too much batter, gently add it straight into the oil. Drizzle some extra batter on top of the cod in the oil. Also make sure there is enough oil for the cod to be fully submerged. Move the cod around so it doesn't stick to the bottom, but don't break the extra crispy chunks off the side. Fry until deep golden brown and crispy, about 3 minutes per side. Set aside on a paper towel–lined plate. Reserve the hot frying oil.

In a medium bowl, add 2 tablespoons of your Nashville Hot mix. Carefully ladle about ¼ cup of your hot frying oil into the bowl and mix.

Butter and toast your buns. Layer a large spoonful of the remoulade sauce on the bottom bun, and from there add the slaw, cod, and then paint on some of your Nashville Hot oil, layer the dill pickles, and finally add more remoulade sauce to your top bun to complete your sandwich. Enjoy!

SERVES: 2

PREP TIME: 10 MIN
PLUS 2 HRS
MARINATING TIME

COOK TIME: 5 MIN

TOTAL TIME:
2 HRS 15 MIN

JOSH WEISSMAN'S BEEF BULGOGI SANDWICH

The text from Josh: "I do have this idea for like a bulgogi ribeye sandwich just littered with fried shallots and a mix of fresh herbs, jalapenos, and a spicy mayo"—Joshua Weissman.

He came over, we made it, and it was insane. It somewhat resembles the flavor of a banh mi, but the fried shallots and chili crisp aioli kick it up a big notch.

FOR THE BEEF BULGOGI

- ½ cup soy sauce
- 1 small pear, sliced
- 3 green onions, roughly chopped
- 3 tablespoons light brown sugar
- 6 garlic cloves, minced
- 1 inch ginger, grated
- 2 tablespoons gochugaru
- 2 tablespoons gochujang
- 2 tablespoons ketchup
- 1 tablespoon mirin (rice wine)
- 1 tablespoon toasted sesame oil
- 1 tablespoon toasted sesame seeds
- 1 teaspoon freshly ground black pepper
- 1 (12-ounce) ribeye steak, very thinly sliced, or shaved with a meat slicer, if possible

FOR THE SANDWICH

- 3 tablespoons garlic chili crisp
- 3 tablespoons Hellmann's or Best Foods mayonnaise
- ½ teaspoon kosher salt
- ½ teaspoon fresh lime juice
- 1 rustic baguette
- ½ cup thinly sliced fresh jalapeños
- 1 cup green onions, thinly sliced lengthwise and placed in a bowl of ice water
- ½ cup packed fresh cilantro roughly chopped with stems
- ½ cup packed fresh mint leaves
- Fried Shallots (page 75)

MAKE THE BULGOGI: In a blender, combine the soy sauce, pear, green onions, brown sugar, garlic, ginger, gochugaru, gochujang, ketchup, mirin, sesame oil, sesame seeds, and pepper. Blend until smooth. Pour the marinade into a freezer bag with your thinly sliced steak and allow to marinate in the refrigerator for 2 to 4 hours.

In a wok over high heat, cook the bulgogi, stirring constantly, until seared, about 5 minutes. Remove from heat.

ASSEMBLE THE SANDWICH: In a small bowl, combine the garlic chili crisp, mayonnaise, salt, and lime juice.

Spread the chili garlic mayo on the bottom of your toasted baguette, followed by a pile of your beef bulgogi, jalapeños, green onions, cilantro, mint, and Fried Shallots, then top it off with the other half of your baguette, also slathered in chili garlic mayo. Enjoy.

JOSH WEISSMAN'S BEEF
BULGOGI SANDWICH,
PAGE 225

BANH MI DIP

Banh mis have a long and interesting history that you should investigate, but here's a SparkNotes version in the meantime. The sandwich is a Vietnamese French fusion recipe dating back to the French colonial period in Vietnam. French soldiers brought baguettes with them, and Vietnamese chefs started mixing pâté with butter and slathering it on the baguettes. Over time different proteins and herbs were added, and the banh mi we know today was born. The dip part I included as a little homage to my trip to Vietnam. I spent a couple months there, and my all-time favorite meal was ordering a banh mi and pho at the same time and dipping the banh mi into the pho broth. When I got back, I started messing around with Vietnamese-inspired au jus for the dip and that's what's in this recipe.

2	large carrots, julienned
1	medium daikon, julienned
2	cups white vinegar
⅔	cup sugar
1	tablespoon kosher salt
2	pounds pork belly
3	tablespoons Cajun seasoning
4	cups beef stock
1	tablespoon hoisin sauce
1	tablespoon beef bouillon base
½	tablespoon fish sauce
1	French baguette
	Whipped Pâté Dip (page 184), for garnish
1	cup julienned green onions
1	cup thinly sliced cucumber
5	Fresno chilis, thinly sliced
1	bunch fresh cilantro
1	bunch fresh mint leaves
	Sriracha, for garnish
2	fresh limes

Take the julienned carrots and daikon and put them in a 32-ounce Mason jar or other heatproof container. In a large pot over high heat, bring the vinegar and 2 cups of water to a boil with the sugar and salt. Pour the liquid over the carrots and daikon until they're fully submerged, then set aside.

Preheat your oven to 300° F.

Shallow-score the pork belly in a ½-inch crosshatch pattern. Season heavily with the Cajun seasoning, then place it on a sheet pan lined with aluminum foil and roast until tender, 2½ hours. More than likely the pork belly won't have the skin on, unless you request otherwise, so you won't get that extra crispy crackling on the outside. Rather, we are looking to hit an internal temp of 185°F to make sure the meat is juicy with rendered fat.

In a large saucepan over medium heat, place your beef stock, hoisin sauce, beef bouillon, and fish sauce. Stir to combine and bring to a gentle boil. Reduce the mixture for 10 minutes, then remove from heat.

CONTINUES

To build your sandwich, toast the baguette in the oven until it's audibly got some crunch on the outside. Cut it lengthwise, almost all the way through, so that it opens like a book. Scoop up a thick layer of the whipped pâté and spread it all over the bottom. Add ½-inch slices of the roasted pork belly, then the green onions, cucumbers, chilis, whole cilantro stems, mint leaves, and a big drizzle of sriracha and a squirt of lime juice.

Serve with a hot bowl of au jus and dip each bite.

BANH MI DIP, CONTINUED

FRENCH DIP

This is probably my favorite recipe—that I've ever come up with. When we began the process of writing this book, this was the first recipe I sent in because it's essentially the most important one in this entire book. Not only because I like it, but because of how many of these techniques can be applied to other dishes. The way I roast this prime rib over onions and use beef stock for the au jus is the same way I roast a turkey over root vegetables and turkey stock for Thanksgiving gravy. The technique I use for the onions is the same one I use for French onion soup. The compound butter I use on the prime rib will make the best garlic bread you've ever had. In fact, most of this recipe is a combination of amazing things I stole from other recipes. It makes sense that those things combined might make one of the top three sandwiches ever created in the history of the world. I know that's bragging, but I seriously think it might be true.

However good it may be, this sandwich is a giant pain in the ass to make, so strap in.

½ cup fresh rosemary sprigs

½ cup fresh thyme sprigs

½ cup fresh oregano

½ cup fresh sage leaves

2 garlic bulbs (cut in half widthwise), plus 8 peeled cloves, divided

½ cup (1 stick) plus 2 tablespoons unsalted butter, divided

1 tablespoon Dijon mustard

2 white onions, sliced in half

2½ pound prime rib roast (2 bone-in ribs)

1 tablespoon flaky salt, plus more for seasoning

1 tablespoon freshly ground black pepper, plus more for seasoning

1 tablespoon extra-virgin olive oil

4 large carrots, peeled and thinly sliced

3 celery stalks, thinly sliced

2 red onions, thinly sliced

3 beef bouillon cubes

8 cups beef stock

½ cup plus 2 tablespoons Worcestershire sauce, divided

1 cup Hellmann's or Best Foods mayonnaise

2 tablespoons prepared horseradish

¼ cup chopped fresh chives

2 large crusty Italian or sourdough baguettes
   Caramelized Onions (page 177)

12 slices provolone cheese

CONTINUES

Preheat the oven to 325°F.

In a blender, place the leaves of the rosemary, thyme, oregano, and sage. Add the 8 peeled garlic cloves and blend to mince. Add the ½ cup (1 stick) of butter cut into cubes and the Dijon mustard. Blend until the butter reaches a soft, whipped consistency and everything is combined.

Place the white onions flat side down on a wire rack–lined roasting dish. Slather the entire roast with the compound butter. Season heavily on all sides with salt and pepper. Place the rib roast on top of the onions, with the top of the roast propped up by the onions and the bottom of the ribs on the wire rack. Roast until the internal temperature of meat reaches 130°F, about 1½ hours. Time may vary so make sure to check the temperature periodically. Remove the meat from roasting dish to rest for 30 minutes.

In a large skillet over medium heat, heat the remaining 2 tablespoons of butter and the olive oil. Add the carrots, celery, sliced red onions, the beef bouillon, the remaining 1 tablespoon of salt, and 1 tablespoon of pepper. Cook, stirring occasionally, until the vegetables are softened and caramelized, about 30 minutes. Add the beef stock, ½ cup of the Worcestershire sauce, and the halved garlic bulbs. Reduce by 40 percent, about 1 hour. Set the halved garlic bulbs aside, then strain the liquid through a fine-mesh sieve, using a large spoon to push all the liquid out of your solids.

Now take the halved garlic bulbs and pop the softened garlic cloves out of their skins. In a medium bowl, mash the softened garlic cloves with the mayonnaise, prepared horseradish, chives, and the remaining 2 tablespoons of Worcestershire sauce, and season to taste with salt and pepper.

While the meat is resting, lightly toast your baguettes.

Using a sharp knife, thinly shave slices of beef from your roast. Slice your baguette in half, and slather your horseradish mayo on the bottom half. On top of that add a large pile of shaved beef, the Caramelized Onions, and slices of provolone. Place both halves under the broiler until the cheese starts to get brown and bubbly. Remove and add more sauce to other half of the bread.

Top your sandwich and cut in half diagonally. Repeat with the remaining baguettes. Serve with hot au jus and enjoy.

BIRRIA DIP

Originally, I made this with Benny Blanco, and that's where he came up with the idea for that zesty-ass avocado salsa. If you don't have time to make the whole sandwich, just whip up that salsa. Guaranteed crowd-pleaser. Also, if you want to make legit birria tacos, you could take the chuck roast recipe and fully do that instead. It's essentially all the same stuff, minus the green salsa, bread, and fried green onions.

1   medium (2-pound) chuck roast
2½   cups vegetable oil, divided
½   tablespoon kosher salt, plus more for seasoning
½   tablespoon freshly ground black pepper, plus more for seasoning
2   white onions, one thinly sliced, one finely diced, divided
12   garlic cloves
10   dried ancho chilis
3   dried guajillo chilis
4   tablespoons dried oregano
12   cups beef stock
1   tablespoon beef bouillon base
½   cup all-purpose flour
½   tablespoon cayenne
½   tablespoon paprika
½   tablespoon garlic powder
½   tablespoon onion powder
6   green onions, thinly sliced lengthwise
1½   cups whole milk
1   rustic baguette
2   cups shredded mozzarella cheese
2   tablespoons extra-virgin olive oil
  Benny Blanco's Avocado Salsa (page 174)
1   cup packed fresh cilantro leaves

Preheat the oven to 325°F.

Cube your chuck roast into 3 x 3-inch pieces. Lather on ½ cup of the vegetable oil, then season very heavily with salt and pepper. Heat 2 tablespoons of the vegetable oil in a Dutch oven over high heat. Sear off the chuck roast pieces on all sides.

Set the chuck roast off to the side and deglaze the pan with 1 thinly sliced onion, the garlic cloves, ancho and guajillo chilis, and oregano. Mix everything, stirring constantly, and make sure to scrape the fond off the bottom, for 2 to 3 minutes. Add the beef stock and bouillon and bring to a boil. Once it's reached a boil, return the chunks of chuck roast to the pot.

Place the Dutch oven, with the lid on, in the oven and cook for 1½ to 2 hours, or until the meat is fall-apart tender.

Remove your chuck roast from the broth and add it to a large bowl. In batches, blend the remaining broth in your Dutch oven until smooth. This will serve as the consommé/jus to dip the sandwich in.

In a medium pot or deep skillet over medium heat, heat the remaining vegetable oil to 350°F.

In a bowl, season the flour with the cayenne, paprika, garlic powder, onion powder, salt, and pepper. Dredge the sliced green onions in the milk and then your seasoned flour. Then, working in batches, fry them until golden brown, 3 to 4 minutes. Immediately season when you remove them to drain on a paper towel–lined sheet pan.

In a large bowl, shred your chuck roast using a couple of forks. Mix in a ladleful of the consommé. Add a pile of chuck roast to your baguette and top it with a handful of mozzarella cheese. Heat a skillet with the olive oil over medium heat and fry the sandwich like a panini.

Once the cheese is melty and the outside of the bread is crispy, open it up and add a heaping handful of your fried green onions and a very large spoonful of your avocado salsa. Also add the diced onions and cilantro to your sandwich and more onions and cilantro to your bowl of consommé for dipping. Enjoy!

BIRRIA DIP, PAGE 234

LAMB BURGER

As mentioned in the Whipped Feta headnote, this burger is my baby. But this baby was conceived by my friend Jerry, so it's a stolen baby. No matter where it came from, this was my first viral recipe and the burger that basically turned my dreams into a reality. Thankfully, it's actually one of the best burgers I've ever made as well. If I had been discovered for some stupid gimmick, I'd probably be stuck doing that. Instead, it's this beautiful lamb burger and now I get to write a cookbook. Once again, totally stole this idea from Jerry, so in a weird butterfly effect way, you guys basically have Jerry to thank for this book existing and for you reading this headnote right now. Thanks, Jerry!

¼   cup harissa paste

¼   cup Hellmann's or Best Foods mayonnaise

1   pound freshly ground lamb
    Flaky salt
    Freshly ground black pepper

1   tablespoon vegetable oil

¼   cup (½ stick) unsalted butter

1   rustic baguette

1½ cups arugula
    Whipped Feta (page 179)
    Pickled Onions (page 191)

In a small bowl, stir together the harissa and mayonnaise. Set aside.

Form the meat into 2 patties and season heavily with flaky salt and pepper on both sides.

Heat the oil in a large skillet over medium to medium-high heat and add the patties, pressing down to ensure full surface coverage. Once they're well seared, about 3 minutes, flip the burgers and add the butter. Basting the burgers continuously, finish cooking to medium rare, about 3 more minutes, and remove.

To build the burger, start by toasting both sides of your baguette. Slather the bottom half with the harissa mayo, then add arugula, burger, a large pile of Whipped Feta, Pickled Onions, and the top of the baguette. Eat!

CHOPPED CHEESE

This is a Harlem staple that most people have never heard of. I'm not gonna compare it to a cheeseburger or a Philly cheesesteak, because it's neither of those. It deserves its own identity rather than being lumped into a combo category. To be fair, if I had to describe it to someone who's never had one, I'd say it's like a Philly cheesesteak mixed with a cheeseburger. BUT I'M NOT GONNA SAY THAT! BECAUSE IT'S A CHOPPED FUCKIN' CHEESE AND DOESN'T COMPARE TO SHIT. I think you'll understand the sentiment after making one. It really does have its own special texture and flavor that the Philly/burger comparison doesn't adequately explain. Once again, shout-out to all the bodegas across Harlem and the rest of Manhattan that brought this sandwich to the world.

1   tablespoon vegetable oil

2   (4-ounce) frozen beef patties

½   cup diced onion

1   teaspoon kosher salt, divided

1   teaspoon freshly ground black pepper, divided

1   teaspoon garlic powder

4   slices American cheese

1   hoagie roll

1   cup shredded lettuce

3   slices tomato

½   cup hot cherry peppers

    Ketchup, for garnish

    Hellmann's or Best Foods mayonnaise, for garnish

To a large cast iron skillet or flat top griddle (*not* nonstick, as you'll be scraping it) over high heat with the vegetable oil, add the beef patties and diced onions. Season heavily with the salt, pepper, and garlic powder and let sear for 2 minutes. Then, using a bench scraper or spatula, start to break all the meat up aggressively until nicely browned and cooked through, 2 to 4 more minutes. You're looking for a ground beef consistency.

Once that's been achieved, form the meat into a sandwich shape and place your slices of cheese on top. Allow the cheese to melt, then chop everything together once more using your spatula. While it's melting, toast your hoagie roll a bit on the side, then scoop the meat and cheese onto the bread. Add the shredded lettuce, tomato, cherry peppers, and season with more salt and pepper. Then squirt some ketchup and mayo to finish it off. Wrap it in parchment paper and cut it in half and serve.

SMASH BURGER

This is just an obligatory recipe for any first-time cookbook author. Once these things hit the internet, they never went away. Entire restaurant chains are being built on the back of this specific burger method, and it's for good reason. It's also for good reason that I didn't leave it out of my book. I don't know who is reading this right now, but if you don't already know how to make a smash burger, you should learn today. If you want make someone happy, make them a smash burger. Don't be conservative with the seasoning, and don't be a wimp when you're smashing it, and this burger will turn out great.

6 ounces 80/20 ground beef

½ teaspoon kosher salt

½ teaspoon freshly ground black pepper

½ teaspoon garlic powder

2 slices American cheese

1 potato bun

1 tablespoon unsalted butter
   Feral Sauce (page 153)

¼ cup sliced red onion, paper-thin

¼ cup sliced pepperoncini

Get a large cast iron skillet ripping hot over high heat. Split your beef into two portions, then form those into 2 balls. Place those balls down on the preheated cast iron skillet. Take a piece of parchment paper and lay it on top of one of the balls. Use a burger press to smash the burger as much as you possibly can and repeat with the other burger.

Season both patties with the salt, pepper, and garlic powder. Once they're well seared, after about 2 minutes, flip your burgers and add your cheese.

While the cheese melts, toast your potato bun in some butter on the side. Once the two halves have formed some color, 1 to 2 minutes, remove them from the heat and add the Feral Sauce to the bottom bun. Add your onion and pepperoncini to the bottom bun.

Stack your patties in the pan, then place them on top of your onion and pepperoncini. Add more burger sauce, top your burger, and enjoy.

STEAK FRITES SANDWICH

Made this sandwich with my boy Laurent and the internet loved it, so here ya go. Once again, we're stealing some recipes from other chapters of this book, so it's a beautiful mutation of items that just make sense together. Steak and fries are an obvious combo, the Horseradish Garlic Mayo never fails in a steak sandwich, and the arugula makes it green and adds a nice peppery flavor. There's really not much to say about this sandwich; it's a glowing representation of the food I like to eat: red meat, sauce, fried shit.

1	(12-ounce) boneless ribeye
2	teaspoons kosher salt
3	tablespoons vegetable oil
¼	cup (½ stick) unsalted butter
1	teaspoon minced garlic
1	sprig fresh rosemary
3	sprigs fresh thyme
1	baguette
	Horseradish Garlic Mayo (page 151), for garnish
	Caramelized Onions (page 177), for garnish
4	slices provolone
	French Fries (page 66)
1½	cups arugula

Season your ribeye heavily with the salt. Get your large cast iron skillet piping hot over high heat and fill the bottom with the oil. Lay your steak in and let it sear for 3 minutes. Flip it over and add your butter, garlic, rosemary, and thyme. Baste until the steak reaches rare to medium rare, an additional 5 minutes. Remove from the skillet and allow to rest for 5 to 10 minutes, then slice into ¼-inch slices.

Preheat the broiler.

Layer the bottom of your baguette with Horseradish Garlic Mayo, sliced steak, Caramelized Onions, and cheese, then throw it under the broiler. On the other side of the bread, add more mayo, then layer fries and arugula. Combine the two halves and enjoy.

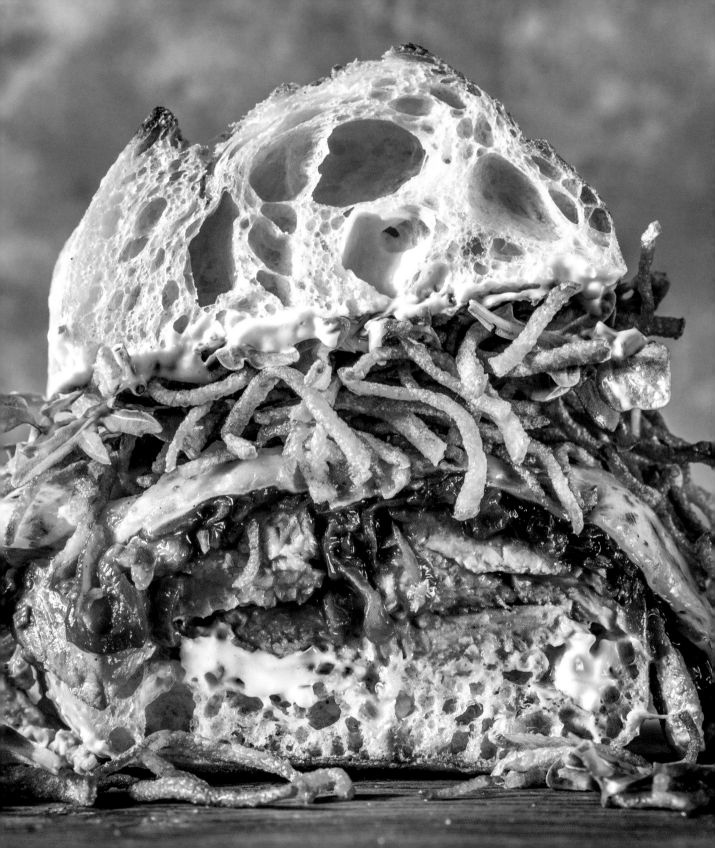

STEAK GRINDER

I wrote this recipe when everyone on TikTok was going viral for making normal grinder sandwiches. I just haaad to be different, but it ended up turning out so good. Honestly, I don't think that's any credit to me; this is just a great sandwich, no matter what meat you put in it. I think adding the giardiniera to the grinder salad might've actually been more rebellious than switching out cold cuts for steak. Either way, this has its own unique flair.

FOR THE GRINDER SALAD

- ½ cup Hellmann's or Best Foods mayonnaise
- 3 tablespoons red wine vinegar
- 2 tablespoons extra-virgin olive oil
- Juice of ½ fresh lemon
- 1 tablespoon dried oregano
- 1 teaspoon kosher salt
- 1 teaspoon freshly ground black pepper
- 1 cup arugula
- 1 cup thinly sliced red onion
- 1 cup Giardiniera (page 192)

FOR THE STEAK

- 3 tablespoons vegetable oil
- 1 (12-ounce) boneless ribeye
- 2 teaspoons kosher salt

FOR THE SANDWICH

- 3 tablespoons garlic compound butter (page 137)
- Crusty Italian baguette
- 1 heirloom tomato, thickly sliced
- Pinch kosher salt
- Pinch freshly ground black pepper
- Balsamic glaze, for garnish
- ½ cup thinly sliced fresh chives, for garnish

MAKE THE GRINDER SALAD: In a large bowl, whisk together the mayonnaise, vinegar, olive oil, lemon juice, oregano, salt, and pepper. Add the arugula, onion, and Giardiniera and toss well.

COOK THE STEAK: In a large cast iron skillet over high heat, heat the oil. Season your steak heavily on both sides, then shallow-fry in your oil until medium rare, 4 minutes on each side. Remove and let rest 5 to 10 minutes, then slice into ¼-inch slices.

ASSEMBLE THE SANDWICH: Preheat the broiler.

Spread the compound butter on both sides of the baguette and broil until toasted.

On the bottom half of the baguette, layer your heirloom tomato slices. Season with salt and pepper. Add a thick layer of the grinder salad, then the sliced steak.

Drizzle balsamic glaze all over your steak, then sprinkle the whole thing with chives. Top your sandwich with the other half of the baguette and eat.

BBQ ROASTED RIB SANDWICH

This sandwich is amazing. It's combining three of our existing recipes, so if you make this entire thing, congratulations, you are officially three recipes deep into this book already (the BBQ sauce, baked ribs, and shoku onion rings).

The pickled slaw is another recipe that could've made the cut as its own recipe. It's one of those things that I genuinely didn't mean to make healthy. You guys know that's not how we do things around here, but it just HAPPENS to have less fat than normal coleslaw and tastes better (in this situation). The slaw recipe can be applied to any number of BBQ sandwiches. It'll cut right through any fatty, meaty ingredients that might be dominating the sandwich, aka ribs and onion rings. BTW, just because this slaw is healthy doesn't mean the sandwich is. This sandwich is, very much so, unhealthy.

1	cup thinly sliced cabbage
1	cup julienned apples
1	cup thinly sliced red onion
3	tablespoons apple cider vinegar
	Juice of 1 fresh lemon
1	teaspoon celery seeds
2	teaspoons kosher salt
2	teaspoons freshly ground black pepper
1	baguette, toasted
	Baked Ribs and BBQ sauce (page 126), for garnish
	Shoku's Caramelized Onion Rings (page 62), for garnish

For the pickled slaw, in a bowl, toss together the cabbage, apples, red onion, cider vinegar, lemon juice, celery seeds, salt, and pepper.

Slather BBQ sauce on the bottom of a toasted baguette, followed by the pickled slaw, deboned ribs, onion rings, and more BBQ sauce, and top off with the other half of the baguette. Eat it up.

INDEX